How I Predicted the Global Economic Crisis*:

The Most Amazing Book You'll Never Read

How I Predicted the Global Economic Crisis*:

The Most Amazing Book You'll Never Read

* and the dot.com collapse, the housing crash, the banking crisis, the stock market plunge, the length and depth of the current recession, the bankrupting of Fannie and Freddie, Europe's debt problems, the muni-bond meltdown, a doubling of gold prices and the even bigger world economic crisis yet to come

John R. Talbott

ISBN: 1-461-01386-0
ISBN-13: 9781461013860

From the Movie - Network (1976)

<u>*Program Director*</u>*: Take 2, cue Howard.*

<u>*Howard Beale (a news anchor speaking into the television camera)*</u>*: I don't have to tell you things are bad. Everybody knows things are bad. It's a depression. Everybody's out of work or scared of losing their job. The dollar buys a nickel's worth; banks are going bust; shopkeepers keep a gun under the counter; punks are running wild in the street, and there's nobody anywhere who seems to know what to do and there's no end to it.*

We know the air is unfit to breathe and our food is unfit to eat. And we sit watching our TVs while some local newscaster tells us that today we had fifteen homicides and sixty-three violent crimes, as if that's the way it's supposed to be!

We all know things are bad -- worse than bad -- they're crazy.

It's like everything everywhere is going crazy, so we don't go out any more. We sit in the house and slowly the world we're living in is getting smaller and all we say is, "Please, at least leave us alone in our living rooms. Let me have my toaster and my TV and my steel-belted radials and I won't say anything. Just leave us alone."

Well, I'm not going to leave you alone. I want you to get mad!

I don't want you to protest. I don't want you to riot. I don't want you to write to your Congressman, because I wouldn't know what to tell you to write. I don't know what to do about the depression and the inflation and the Russians and the crime in the street.

All I know is that first, you've got to get mad.

You've gotta say, "I'm a human being, goddammit! My life has value!"

So, I want you to get up now. I want all of you to get up out of your chairs. I want you to get up right now and go to the window, open it, and stick your head out and yell,

"I'm as mad as hell, and I'm not going to take this anymore!!"

Howard Beale
Played by Peter Finch
Awarded the Oscar for Best Performance by an Actor posthumously
Written by Paddy Chayefsky
Directed by Sidney Lumet
Metro Goldwyn Mayer (MGM)

When I despair, I remember that all through history the way of truth and love has always won. There have been tyrants and murderers and for a time they seem invincible, but in the end, they always fall -- think of it, ALWAYS.

M.K. Gandhi

All Good People

Lyrics to the song by the musical group Yes
Written by Jon Anderson - 1971

*I´ve seen all good people turn their heads each day so satisfied I´m
on my way.*
*I´ve seen all good people turn their heads each day so satisfied I´m
on my way.*

Take a straight and stronger course
To the corner of your life.
Make the white queen run so fast
She doesn´t have time to make you a wife.

*´Cause it´s time, it´s time in time with your time and its news is
captured*
For the queen to use.

Move me onto any black square.
Use me any time you want.
Just remember that the goal
´Sfar as us is t´capture all we want.

Don´t surround yourself with yourself.
Move on back two squares.
Send an instant karma to me:
Initial it, with loving care.

*´Cause it´s time, it´s time in time with your time and its news is
captured*
For the queen to use.

*I´ve seen all good people turn their heads each day so satisfied I´m
on my way.*
*I´ve seen all good people turn their heads each day so satisfied I´m
on my way.*

About the Author

John R. Talbott is the bestselling author of eight books on economics and politics that have accurately detailed and predicted the causes and devastating effects of this entire financial crisis including, in 2003, *The Coming Crash in the Housing Market*. In 2004, he correctly identified corporate and banking lobbyists and big corporate money in politics as the major underlying cause of the current crisis with, *Where America Went Wrong*. In January 2006, he called the absolute peak month of home prices in the US by releasing, *Sell Now! The End of the Housing Bubble* and warned that the problem was not local, or even national, but international. In 2008, his book, *Contagion: The Financial Epidemic That Is Sweeping the Global Economy* predicted the subprime mortgage problem developing in the US would mutate and grow and infect not only prime mortgages, but other markets such as the stock market, commercial real estate, the municipal bond market, as well as threaten the solvency of banks and governments around the globe leading to a very long, deep and painful global recession. In 2009, *The 86 Biggest Lies on Wall Street* exposed the ineptness of the government's response to the crisis and the futility of enacting real reform of Wall Street when Wall Street itself is the biggest lobbyist of our congress.

Formerly, an investment banker for Goldman Sachs and a Visiting Scholar at UCLA's Anderson School of Management, Talbott has written peer reviewed academic research on democracy, inequality, AIDS prevention and developing country economics and has acted as an economic adviser to Jordan and Russia. He has made presentations on economics and politics throughout the United States and in Italy and Australia. He graduated from Cornell's School of Engineering and received an MBA from UCLA. His work has appeared in the Wall

Street Journal, the Financial Times, the Boston Globe, the San Francisco Chronicle, the Herald Tribune, the New Republic, the Huffington Post and salon.com. He has appeared as a financial expert on television for CNN, CBS, Fox News, CNBC, FBN, CSPAN and MSNBC as well as on hundreds of radio programs. Talbott, whose family has lived in Kentucky for 230 years is the son of a career Army officer, is 56 years old, single, an avid college football and basketball fan and lives with his faithful companion, Boca Jr., who rarely objects to any of Talbott's writings or politics except when it is time to go for a walk.

The media can contact Talbott at johntalbs@gmail.com as well as anyone who might be interested in discussing possible speaking engagements. As usual, he looks forward to hearing from you, the reader and will try to respond personally to all of your emails, postcards and letters.

This book is dedicated to the tens of millions of families around the world who are needlessly suffering from losing their jobs, their homes and their savings to a global economic crisis that never had to happen.

And to my mentors: Findley Meislahn, Dick Roll, Peter Fahey, Fred Eckert, Bill Talbott, Daron Acemoglu and Ed Leamer

Books by John R. Talbott

Slave Wages: How the Rich and Powerful
    Play the Game (1999)

The Coming Crash in the Housing Market (2003)

Where America Went Wrong (2004)

Sell Now! The End of the Housing Bubble (2006)

Obamanomics (2008)

Contagion: The Financial Epidemic That Is Sweeping
    the Global Economy (2008)

The 86 Biggest Lies on Wall Street (2009)

How I Predicted the Global Economic Crisis:
    The Most Amazing Book You'll Never Read (2011)

Table of Contents

A Note from the Author

The most amazing book you'll never read? What's so amazing about this book? You'll see in the table of contents that much of it was written long before the beginning of the current economic crisis. In fact, a great deal of this book is composed of excerpts from my previous writings over the last twelve years. And yet there is an incredible amount still to be learned from this work that has as much applicability and relevance today as it did then. What is amazing is that as you read these chapters you will scarce believe when they were written. For you see, for reasons even I don't completely understand, I have been incredibly prescient in my ability to predict the events of our current economic crisis long before they actually occurred. And I believe I got the causal mechanics correct as well.

Sure, I have made some minor mistakes in my prophesies, but not many. I hope in reading this book you find yourself while reading, turning back to the beginning of the chapters to confirm the date on which they were written. Like I say, it is pretty amazing. Even I am amazed as I was taught at business school that no one can predict the economic future in normal times, and I believed it then and I believe it now, but these are not normal times.

My suggestion that this is a book that you will never read comes from a number of simple facts. One, the average American reads less than one book per year. That alone is a pretty amazing statistic. Does this mean that the average American can't finish even a good murder mystery? We have become a nation of television viewers and Internet surfers with little time to settle in with a good book. I, of course, am a little biased being an author, but I believe this one fact alone explains to a great degree why America's democratic institutions and the very foundations of our economy have been so threatened without greater public outrage. If people don't read non-fiction books, they don't learn how to critically think, they are uninformed and they depend on others to package the news and form opinions for them. If they don't read novels they never learn empathy, the ability to put yourself in someone else's shoes. They never learn life's ethical lessons on the fictitious practice fields of novels, but rather have to learn them in the much less forgiving real world game of life.

Two, the book is about economics. Thanks to the graph-filled introductory economic courses many of us took in school, the mere mention of the word economics causes our eyelids to become heavy and to start to flutter and close. I try in the book to tailor my comments to the non-economist layman, and based on readers' comments of my previous books I think I have been successful. At times, I am sure I get deeper into economic reasoning than many of you would prefer me to. One, forgive me for indulging one of my true loves and two, please realize that if some of this is difficult for you to read, it still might be good for you to read it. I believe people have to acquire a minimal level of competence in economics and finance or they are setting themselves up for being ripped off by others who have made a career of its study. In today's world, it is not sufficient for citizens to be good students of civics, they also must understand how economics drives many of the political and societal decisions we make today.

Another reason you may choose not to read this book is that you find you are just worn out, burned out, sick of thinking about not only the depressing aspects of this economic crisis but also the incredibly depressing lapses in ethics and the criminality that caused it. Again, I am right with you. I find this all incredibly depressing. Imagine it from my perspective. You've been thinking about it since its outbreak in 2006. I've been thinking and writing about it since 1999. Whoever said ignorance is bliss had it right. On one hand, it is incredibly rewarding to be able to predict these events before they happen. On the other, think how frustrating it is to see a train wreck coming and to be unable to do anything to stop it.

With regard to your symptoms of burnout, all I can say is please stick with it. It isn't over yet. The worst may indeed be yet to come. Without your involvement, it certainly will. Why should you invest time in something that is difficult and can make you sad rather than happy? It is the same reason I write about it. Because we are concerned about others; it is our cross to bear. Life is not just about maximizing happiness. It is mostly about leading fulfilling lives. And nothing can be more fulfilling than working together to find a solution to the systemic problems that are causing such suffering and pain to tens of millions of people on this planet.

The final reason you may not read this book is the same reason why many of you have not read my previous books. Even though I have sold hundreds of thousands of books and appeared before millions on television and radio you may not know my story. I know I am not a household name. And before the crisis unfolded, I can understand why many either didn't hear or ignored my warnings. But now that the crisis has unfolded exactly as I foretold, I do start to wonder why the media has not sought me out for my opinions on needed reforms as well as my expectations of what comes next.

I started to come to the conclusion that maybe I wasn't as funny as I thought I was. Maybe I wasn't a good guest on radio and television. Even though I had been told numerous times that I was, maybe they say that to all their guests. And then I went to Australia.

I went to Australia for 10 days to promote a new book I had written in 2009. I expected to give a short talk at the Brisbane Writers Festival and make a couple of bookstore appearances in Sydney and Melbourne and be done. Well, I became a media darling. They had me on national television two or three times a day and on the radio three or four times each day. And they loved me. It turns out I was funny and entertaining. And I had something to say.

My main message, that big corporations and banks have come to dominate our lives, control our politics and was the prime reason for the current economic crisis was warmly received in Australia by audience members as well as my media hosts. What is difference between Australia's media and media in the United States? Approximately half of Australia's media, including its radio and television is publicly owned. It seems like Rupert Murdoch owns the rest, but I am sure this is an oversimplification. In the United States, more than 90% of the media is privately owned and the vast majority of that by corporations.

Trust me, I am not being paranoid when I tell you that the major cable and network television shows in the United States, as well as our major newspapers were not excited by me spreading this anti-corporate message. While corporate lobbying excesses are the basis of almost all of my books, when I appeared on television programs I was never asked about it. One time, a producer stopped me minutes before I was due to go on his show, pointed to a chart in one of my books that listed the country's largest corporate lobbyists and the billions of dollars of tax breaks they were receiving because of it and said, you have to come back on again and talk about this. This is dynamite. He never called again.

One of my book publishers, who is one of the largest publishers in the world, straight out told me that if I did not revise my chapter on corporate lobbying abuse they would publish my book as required by our contract, but they wouldn't promote it. They would let it die on the vine. They wanted three pages of discussion about lobbying removed from the book. I refused and a book which had taken me 1 1/2 years to write, edit and publish was released by my publisher with no public announcement, no press release, no advertising support, no book tour and no television or radio appearances. I don't think it sold 5,000 copies, incredible given that another book I had written just nine months before sold close to 80,000 copies and generated hundreds of radio and TV appearances. This is how censorship works in America. Nobody comes to your house in the dark of night with a club threatening you or telling you what to write. But if what you write is not appealing to the large corporate-owned publishing houses, it never sees the light of day. It gets put in the back of the book stores and gets lost with what may be the other 100,000 books corporate America didn't approve of. As Billy Joes says, I got put in the back on the discount rack like another can of beans.

That is why I am taking a different tack with this book. Although I have a successful record as a bestselling author, I have decided to self publish this book rather than depend on any of the big corporate-owned publishing houses. I will emphasize e-book sales and do most of my promotion work through the Internet. Hopefully, this will become a model for all authors in the future that will allow us to get closer to our readers without the uncalled for censorship and intervention of large corporate publishers.

So if you've made it this far, hopefully you will read this book. I think I can honestly say you won't be disappointed. I was thinking about including a money back guarantee if you read the book in its entirety and can honestly say you didn't learn anything of value. I guess I will honor that guarantee as I am highly confident that you will enjoy the book.

You might ask how it is that I was able to make accurate predictions about our economic future when so many professional economists clearly got it wrong. I believe my situation is unique. As they say, sometimes it is better to be lucky than to be smart and I lucked into having an ideal background for doing this work. I worked for 10 years on Wall Street as an investment banker for Goldman Sachs, back when that was an honorable profession, so I understand derivatives, credit default swaps and CDOs, something many economists didn't comprehend at the time of the crisis.

But I left Wall Street to study and do academic research on how corruption prevented developing countries from prospering. I thought I could make corrupt and oligarchic Argentina more like the United States. Little did I know that the United States was becoming more like Argentina.

But my study of Africa and Latin America and the Middle East left me with a clear understanding of how damaging corruption and oligarchies can be to a democracy and to an economy. My co-author, Dick Roll and I wrote the definitive research paper on how civil liberties, a free press and the vote make for good government and a healthy, growing economy. Today, the best writing by academics about the financial crisis we are suffering from are from economists like Simon Johnson and Daron Acemoglu who are not specialists in derivatives or finance, but rather are experts in the field of developing country economics. They know how fragile our institutions are to corruption and they explain beautifully the dangers of allowing all political and economic decisions to be made by a few wealthy individuals or powerful corporations, lessons they learned from studying the developing world.

I had one other great advantage that most economists studying this problem did not. My brother Bill teaches philosophy at the University of Washington and he spent six months on the telephone with me teaching me about the foundations of ethical institutions and collective action problems. I will let you read this book to learn more about collective action problems, but I can tell you they are one of the key causes of the entire financial crisis. Collective action problems are situations in which the best outcome for all participants is reached through cooperation rather than competition. The unregulated free markets unleashed on us by Ronald Reagan and Milton Friedman excel at solving traditional economic pricing and distribution problems, but have no comprehension of how to approach or find a solution to a collective action problem.

The final reason why I believe I was successful in predicting these dire economic events is that I am completely independent. I left Wall Street 20 years ago and never looked back. I support myself solely through my writing and have no corporate sponsors, bosses, management committees or boards to report to. Simply, I am not conflicted. I try very hard to seek the truth and when I find it, I write about it. I have never cared about who might be harmed from my exposés, I have always believed that seeking the truth is the best policy.

So that partly explains why I was uniquely positioned to predict these crises over the last 12 years. You might also ask, why did tens of thousands of professional economists around the world get it so wrong? The Keynesians missed it, the libertarians missed it, the behavioralists missed it (with the exception of Robert Shiller who got it right, but I think for the wrong reasons), the monetarists missed it, the macro crowd missed it, the Chicago boys missed it, the freshwater and saltwater economists missed it, the Harvard crowd missed it, the Wall Street crowd missed it, the Federal Reserve missed it, White House advisors missed it and the corporate media's economic pundits completely missed it.

I believe economists today suffer from a number of various serious problems in their profession. They have become, as a group, overly technical and mathematical in their pursuit of the truth. While attempting to become ever more precise and specialized in their knowledge, they have lost the ability to see the big picture and to think outside their narrow area of expertise. And if they had to choose between their theoretical or empirical models and actual feedback and facts from the real world, they seem to always choose their models over reality. Math is pure. Math is certain. Math has proofs. The real world is much messier. Proofs and certainty are impossible. All we can do is strive to chase the truth and someday hopefully touch its coattails.

Second, many of the economists and finance professors who should have seen this crisis coming, such as those specializing in mortgage markets, banking, derivatives, options and capital markets faced an incredible potential conflict of interest. Many of the top professors in these fields were being paid multiples of their teaching salaries from the very hedge funds, private equity groups, commercial banks and investment banks that were at the center of this crisis. Most professors are allowed by their universities to spend one day a week working in the real world in their field of expertise. This led many finance professors to work as consultants, expert witnesses and partners to many of the largest firms on Wall Street. I believe it was this obvious financial conflict of interest that prevented many of these very smart individuals from speaking out prior to the crisis erupting. Today, I am even more certain of this belief as I see very few academics speaking out on the need for significant reform to how Wall Street is regulated. It is sad that Simon Johnson is carrying the entire burden for an academic universe that is too conflicted, even now, after the fact, to speak out against the banking industry.

Of course, many economists had one other great disadvantage in seeing this crisis coming. They shared a group think mentality that unregulated free markets were the solution to all of our problems. They believed that markets never failed. That regulation was not only unnecessary, but undesirable. That regulation got in the way of markets efficiently finding the proper prices to achieve the greatest increases of welfare for the people. That markets were right, and if not right, were as close as we could come to right. That asset bubbles couldn't exist because that would mean markets had gotten it wrong with regard to pricing of assets. And if bubbles couldn't happen, then we didn't have to worry about market crashes and corrections either. And that corporations and their executives, acting in their narrow self interest for bigger profits and bonuses determined a path that was best for society as a whole and for its citizens. This book will demonstrate my love of capitalism as a force for productive good, but will also discuss its limits as a societal force, especially when we allow corporations out of the economic marketplace and into the political arena.

So I hope you enjoy this compilation of my previous work, along with new chapters I have written for this book. I have tried to include what I thought were the best portions of my prior work. I apologize to bloggers who rarely read anything that wasn't written in the last five minutes, but I do believe in this case recent history has a lot to teach us. Until we understand the real causes of this crisis we will not emerge from it, nor will we be prepared for the even larger crisis yet to come that I discuss in the last chapter.

As always, I will not consider this a success unless it first gets you depressed, then gets you angry and finally gets you motivated to get involved in the struggle to end corporate dominance of our government, our society and our lives. Enjoy!

John R. Talbott
March 15, 2011
johntalbs@gmail.com

Chapter 1

Written in February 1999

Selected Excerpts from *Slave Wages: How the Rich and Powerful Play the Game*

Following are selected excerpts from "Slave Wages: How the Rich and Powerful Play the Game", a book Talbott wrote and published in February 1999.

<u>*Do You Hear The People Sing?*</u>

From the musical "Les Miserables"
Music by Alain Boublil and Claude-Michel Schönberg
Lyrics by Herbert Kretzmer
Based on the book by Victor Hugo

Will you join in our crusade?
Who will be strong and stand with me?
Beyond the barricade
Is there a world you long to see?
Then join in the fight
That will give you the right to be free!

Will you give all you can give
So that our banner may advance
Some will fall and some will live
Will you stand up and take your chance?
The blood of the martyrs
Will water the meadows of France!

Do you hear the people sing?
Singing a song of angry men?
It is the music of a people
Who will not be slaves again!
When the beating of your heart
Echoes the beating of the drums
There is a life about to start
When tomorrow comes!

The Real Cause of Recessions

The later years of the 20th century have witnessed a dramatic victory of free-market capitalism over state-sponsored communism. Communism was no match for the brute power and efficiency of a free-market system. Substantial growth and technological advancements have occurred under capitalism. Great fortunes have been amassed during capitalism's reign. And yet, to those of us living in the United States, in one of the most free of the free-market economies, something feels amiss. There are great numbers of people who are not sharing in the vast rewards of our capitalist system, but given the overall success of the free market system, we are hesitant to criticize.

Even those of us who realize that there is a fundamental problem residing in the free market system have difficulty describing exactly what that problem might be. We do not know if the problem reflects a fundamental flaw in the theory of free-market economics, results from a special type of problem that free-market systems are ill-equipped to handle, results from some type of dislocation affecting the model due to current circumstances or is a result of certain violations of the basic assumptions behind free-market economic theory.

Often, when our economy has troubles and falls into recession, the first one blamed is the worker. Complaints vary but include worker laziness, lack of productivity on the job, inefficient work rules, overly powerful unions or a minimum wage that is too high. I find most of these complaints laughable. American households are working harder, longer, more productively and for lower wages than they ever have before.

We shall examine in detail the real causes of the economic troubles that face our country. We shall see that the real culprits causing our recessions, depressions, inflationary spirals, real wage declines, major business collapses, unemployment and growth stagnation are not our hard-working people, but rather, a very powerful combination of our largest corporations, our commercial banks and our governmental institutions that are more interested in responding to the lobbying of big money special-interests than in providing to the needs of their people.

We shall see that even our study of economics is biased by these big money special interests. One could argue that we are not even measuring and tracking the proper economic statistics. The country's focus on GDP growth and the performance of the Dow Jones

Industrial Average may be improperly measuring or ignoring the quality of life of its average citizens. Such a focus on corporate profits and general overall growth of the economy can prevent an understanding of how the average American working man and woman are doing.

In this era of unbounded world capitalism, with free markets being more unconstrained than ever, it is important to remind ourselves of the limits of capitalism in solving problems that the free-market is ill equipped to address.

People today seem so enamored with the free market as a God-sent solution to all their problems that I think I will have added a little value if I can convince you that it alone will not get us out of this situation.

Other Causes of Recessions

There is a cause of recessions in our country and around the world in addition to a government's monetary policy. It is caused by a large institution, not by the actions of the citizens of the country. In this case the guilty institution is the commercial bank. I have seen in my lifetime many examples of this problem. In general, the problem begins with the commercial bank getting into trouble with a certain sector of its loan portfolio. For a number of reasons including mismanagement, poor credit analysis or over-aggressiveness, commercial banks often get in a position where they begin to have significant loan losses in a particular segment of their lending. I have seen this in the United States in many different areas. In the early 80's, the banks overextended themselves in farm lending. Later in the decade they loaned way too much money on far too aggressive terms to real estate developers. During the late 80's they loaned too much money to corporations in the form of leveraged buyouts. These bank problems led directly to the country's recession in 1990. More recently, the U.S. commercial banks got caught with their pants down in their international lending to countries such as Korea, Thailand, Malaysia, Indonesia, Russia and Brazil.

The excesses were legendary. Office buildings were being built in this country with 100% bank debt and no equity. Leveraged buyouts were being structured at such high prices that there was no means forecasted of paying current interest and no ability imagined to pay back principal. Domestic and foreign loans were being extended to the largest Korean companies until their debt loads were equal to eight and nine times their equity. Debt represented more than 80% of the total capitalization of the average large Korean company in 1997.

At the first small sign of trouble, you can imagine what the U.S. commercial bank's reaction was. It ran, not walked, to the nearest exit. Not only did the bank cease all new loans in the sector; it did everything it could to reduce its exposure to the industry, sector or country. In plain English, this meant calling in loans. Banks extend credit subject to very long and complex covenant agreements. Anytime, especially during difficult times, it is common for a borrower to be in technical default on some of these covenants, allowing the bank to call the loan, thus forcing the borrower to repay the loan in full, on demand. One can imagine how devastating this would be to a business that had assumed that its bank debt represented long-term capital. Companies, farmers, even countries have sufficient income each year to pay the interest due on a bank loan, but do not keep the funds available to immediately repay the entire principal. Proceeds from the bank loans are tied up in illiquid assets, such as buildings, farm machinery, equipment, etc. Because banks reduce their exposure across an entire sector all at once, they force borrowers to sell illiquid assets, under fire-sale conditions, into an already overcrowded buyers market.

Sometimes banks' lending practices are so poor that their bad loans are not restricted to one particular sector of the economy. Sometimes, bad loans at banks get to be such a significant percentage of the bank's assets that it threatens the very existence of the bank. Remember, banks are leveraged with debt themselves, approximately 20 to 1. This means that for every $1 of equity capital, the bank has $20 of debt on its balance sheet. If 5% of the bank's loans go bad and are not repaid, it can wipe out 100% of the bank's equity. This should result in the bank's bankruptcy, but knowing this, the bank might be very slow to disclose its problems to regulators and the public.

Instead, the bank pulls back from lending on a worldwide basis, affecting every sector of our economy and the world economy. In fact, the bank stops all new lending. Since a bank is in the business of lending, you might ask what it does when it decides not to issue new loans. What does it invest in? The answer is it holds risk-free debt securities, such as U.S. Treasury securities. It borrows under very short-term debt arrangements and invests in longer-term Treasuries. It then creates risk-free profits on the spread between its borrowing costs and the yield on the Treasury securities. It maintains this position for a sufficient enough time period for the profits to replenish its depleted equity capital base.

Bank capital is such an important ingredient in the formation of all new economic enterprises that when it is restricted its impact is devastating. No new construction of office buildings, no bank-financed expansion of factories and other corporate facilities, no growth financing for small businesses, etc. Commercial banks have the ability to absolutely obliterate what was an otherwise healthy economy. The shortsightedness of this approach is only surpassed by the cruelty of its impact on our civilian workforce. Unemployment skyrockets, not due to any corporate inefficiency or labor slowdown, but rather because a commercial banker made some very poor decisions in extending credit to his customers.

The Limits of Free-Market Capitalism

For a number of years, there has been a very strong movement among conservatives in this country to eliminate all governmental interference and let the free markets operate completely freely. These libertarians believe that any and all interference by the government in a free-market system is inappropriate and leads to a less than optimal allocation of resources.

These people do not understand that free markets require involvement by the government in order to provide a framework in which free markets can operate. Free-markets assume that exchanges occur between individuals without coercion. The government is needed to assure that contracts are honored, that no coercion has occurred and that a justice system has been developed to punish any transgressors.

Clearly, in our country, our system of government and justice has been in place for so long that we've begun to take it for granted. Yes, our government has gotten a bit bloated and inefficient. If one finds distasteful its cumbersome regulations, its intrusiveness and its inefficiency, one should also not lose sight of the essential nature of good government.

In addition to the basic governmental supervision requirements that are needed for free markets to operate, there are a few situations that capitalistic free markets are ill suited to handle. In general, many fit what are called collective action problems. We shall see that they all share a common structure, but that they are very diverse in terms of the products, services and markets that are affected.

Collective-action problems are defined as situations in which participants, each acting in their own self-interest decide on a course of action that from each of their perspectives maximizes value to himself, but ignores a solution involving possible cooperation between them that, if chosen, would be more beneficial to all relative to the alternative of not cooperating.

A simple example is one's decision to litter. Any individual, if only thinking of his own self-interest, can decide that his littering is all right because it alone is not significant enough to damage the environment. If the environment is pristine, his small amount of littering will have little effect, and if the environment is filthy, a little bit more couldn't hurt. The problem results when all the citizens in town take this same approach and begin to litter. If, however, all the citizens cooperate and all agree not to litter, all will be better off. Building these consensus solutions in collective action problems is difficult because individuals must look past their immediate self-interest, something a free market is not equipped well to handle. Free markets are based on the assumption that everyone, and here I mean each and every individual, will act in his own self-interest and that this will lead to an optimal solution. In collective action problems, without cooperation by the participants, a less than optimal solution is attained.

A second common characteristic involved in all collective action problems is that they all have the potential problem of allowing "free riders". Free riders are those individuals in the group who do not participate in the costs of the collective solution but passively receive the benefits. The person who litters is a free rider because he enjoys a relatively clean environment created by the cooperation of others and, yet, he does not do his part in helping keep the environment clean. The ability to punish free riders is important for the long-term success of any collective action solution.

There are a number of other shortcomings of the capitalist free market system which deserve mention which may not be as concrete and as easily defined as collective action problems. I believe participants in a free-market economy feel them and can describe them, but to date no economist has adequately created a theory that explains them.

Free market systems seem to have a volatility at certain times that is far greater and seems to reflect some other phenomenon than just new information coming into the marketplace. At times it seems that investors have lost confidence in an entire sector of the market and that this loss of confidence becomes a self-fulfilling prophecy as it leads to a market catastrophe. Often free-market theorists do not appreciate that such an ephemeral quality as confidence can have such a meaningful impact on the hard valuation of assets, which they like to determine through present value analysis.

Why is it that confidence plays such an important role in the free markets? I would argue that the introduction of leverage, i.e., the use of short-term debt financing rather than equity financing by governments, financial institutions and companies to fund their operations creates a situation in which confidence is all important. Any country, bank or company that has issued short-term debt and spent the proceeds on longer-term assets, such as buildings and equipment, is assuming that the debt investors will all have sufficient confidence such that they will not all demand repayment at once. Many longer-term assets do not have sufficient liquidity such that they could be sold on short notice for fair value.

In a leveraged society there are numerous examples of confidence-type problems. Every time we spend a U.S. dollar, the recipient has the confidence to know that the piece of paper has worth. It is backed by the good faith and credit of the United States, but the United States does not have the gold reserves to redeem every note. Each commercial bank, as we have seen, has only $1 of equity capital for every $15 to $20 of debt capital. If everybody in the country removed the entire balance from their checking account on the same day, the banks would collapse. Most corporations could not repay all of their short-term debt without dramatically shrinking their business. Many developing countries can face a similar crisis of confidence when many foreign banks and investors all decide to withdraw funds on the same day.

Maybe these confidence games explain the high degree of volatility in the valuations of a developing country's assets during difficult economic times. Although the outlook for the country may not have changed materially, the actions of an international bank or consortium of foreign banks may spell disaster to the developing country. Investors must not only weigh the prospects of the country's economy deteriorating, they must also assign a probability to a currency devaluation or to a capital flight. Cooperation among banks and investors to prevent such a capital flight is subject to collapse if enough parties defect from that cooperation and flee the country. Country and company debts exacerbate the problem because the first to lose confidence and flee is rewarded by being repaid in full, while those that cooperate and stay have the greatest risk of losing part or all of their investment.

Capitalism's emphasis on money leads to what is probably the most popular criticism of capitalism, that it emphasizes greed. Defenders of capitalism are quick to point out that greed is important for survival in any competitive environment and that humans have probably been biologically selected through evolution to be greedy. I don't think capitalism causes greed, but living in a market economy day-in and day-out clearly reinforces it. It is one thing to want to compete aggressively to make a better product, but quite a different matter if one's greed leads him to destroy his professional, personal and family relationships in chasing the almighty dollar. Governor Cuomo of New York said it best, "Survival of the fittest is a fine theory to describe the evolution of animals, but it is a poor model to use as a basis of a society."

Recently, capitalism as practiced in our country has led to a very great disparity between our country's richest and poorest. I believe this is a direct result of allowing free-market capitalism to run unfettered. Historians will compare this period in our history with the early 20th century, when capitalism was unbounded and monopolies and trusts ruled.

There have been many attempts to explain how the majority of the wealth created recently has ended up in the hands of our richest citizens. I believe it is a direct result of the oversupply of labor in the world environment and its impact on depressing wages. The end of communism has opened new markets for our goods and at the same time provided a large pool of underutilized labor. The growth and profit potential from this combination are enormous.

Capitalism rewards growth. Growth is most easily accomplished through rapid technological change. Clearly, there are enormous benefits to technological change. We citizens, however, are not choosing to live in this world of hyper-growth. Our economic system, with its bias towards growth, has chosen it for us. Uncontrolled growth brings with it an enormously stressful environment, environmental degradation and an inability for the less technologically sophisticated to adjust accordingly. Technology is advancing so rapidly that individuals are facing obsolescence in the workplace in their early 40's. Whom does this growth really benefit? Obviously growth is a major component in determining valuations in the stock market.

Given that we all must endure the hardships that super normal growth entails, we should all have a say in the amount of growth we wish to see in our economy. Many people's wishes for a simpler time and a simpler life are steamrolled by an economic system that does not understand and puts no value on such stability. Because such comments are so "uneconomic," they are dismissed before getting a fair hearing. We have fallen so in love with our free-market system that we are quick to dismiss any idea that might be good for our society but is a detriment to the performance of that economic system. We must recognize that we, as individuals, have values that a free-market system cannot put a price on.

There is another problem that is created by the rapid growth and rapid change in a constantly improving and increasingly efficient free-market system. One can imagine how difficult it is to do anything in an advanced free-market system that really creates value. All one has to do to create value is to think of a better mousetrap, but eventually, most of the mousetraps have already been thought of. One's employer and his stockholders are no less demanding. They insist on generating ever increasingly large profits. This puts employees under enormous pressure to take shortcuts and perform unethically. We all shake our heads when corporations or employees of corporations are caught doing such unethical and sometimes illegal activities but we really should understand that we have created an economic system which places enormous pressures on the individual to perform miracles in an increasingly more difficult and tougher environment. I do not mean to excuse such ethical lapses, but I do want to point out the free-market system's culpability as a co-conspirator in the transgression.

Such pressures on individuals and corporations lead to what I call "bad profits." As opposed to the good profits that result from an exchange of goods or services in which both parties benefit, bad profits result when one of the parties acts unethically to exploit or take advantage of the other party. Examples range from situations as simple as someone selling a used car that he knows has undisclosed problems, to major manufacturers selling what they know are unsafe products and then doing everything in their power to hide the effects from the public and avoid legal liability. What are the motivations of people who work for or own shares in tobacco companies? What kind of individual could design weapons that cause massive injuries and death to the human population? Why would an individual want to own or run a company that exploited its workforce and forced them to live in squalid conditions? Why would someone lie in order to cheat another person in a business dealing? The answer; Because it is profitable.

Corporations were supposedly formed to limit the amount of personal liability that owners had and, thus, protect their personal assets. I believe that the corporate form also allows one to protect his own personal ethical identity. I believe that unethical actions are often taken by employees, managers, executives and shareholders in the name of their corporation that these individuals would never undertake personally if their own personal reputation were at stake. They conveniently have separated in their minds their own personal self-image and ethical responsibilities from the actions they undertake on behalf of the corporation. They may be deceiving themselves in this creation, but I believe the deception is often necessary in order to successfully compete in an always more competitive economic environment. They act unethically in order to sell more product, but they end up selling their souls.

Capitalism's continued emphasis on consumerism leads to a credit-based society. Home mortgages, car loans, credit cards, installment purchases, personal loans, bank loans, home equity loans are all encouraged by a society that wishes to see consumption spending rise today rather than tomorrow. Many commercial banks currently experience default rates in excess of 5% on their credit-card portfolio. Because they charge 18% on outstanding balances, this still nets them an attractive profit. This is the next great loan loss debacle facing our banks. If they are comfortable with a 5% default rate in their credit card portfolios during the longest peacetime economic expansion in our country's history, what are their expectations for the default rate if a recession occurs?

These banks are little concerned with the grief they create for families who destroy their good credit ratings or claim personal bankruptcy. If Nathaniel Hawthorne had written *The Scarlet Letter* today, the letter emblazoned on certain of our citizens would not be an A for adulterer, but would be the letters LC for lousy credit. In an era of instant communications and sophisticated computers, a person's bad credit report follows him everywhere and impacts everything he tries to do. Of course, I am not encouraging people to spend more than they have, but in a leveraged society, knee deep in debt and with no assurance of lifetime employment, job interruptions can lead to unexpected cash problems. Additionally, it is almost impossible to have any misleading item on one's credit report corrected. As is typical of most of the items discussed here, this problem primarily affects the working class. Everything seems to be done to protect the merchant, but little is done to protect the consumer. I believe the unfairness and the intrusiveness of credit reporting is one of the areas that the average working person in our country finds most objectionable.

Such are some of the problems associated with letting a free-market economy run wild. We shall see that a critical component in controlling the excesses of a free-market economy lie in a government that responds more to its electorate than to a big money lobbying effort on behalf of big business.

Excess and Collapse

There are numerous examples in recent history of extreme collapses of businesses and sometimes entire industry sectors that are so spectacular and so costly that one wonders whether the free market might be completely out of control. The free market allows for an evolutionary regeneration that includes some bankruptcies of inefficient producers, but one would hope that this process could occur in an orderly manner without threatening the economy's well being, and quite possibly, the entire economic system.

The list of just some of these spectacular collapses that I have witnessed in my adult lifetime is rather long. It includes:

The collapse of the S&L industry in the 1980's

The U.S. stock market collapse, known as Black Monday, in October 1987.

The collapse in 1990 of Drexel Burnham, Mike Milken and their junk-bond empire.

The explosion of bankruptcies in the leveraged buyout field in the early 90's.

The unfortunate demise (and more unfortunate rebirth) of Donald Trump and his real-estate empire in the early 90's.

The commercial real-estate debacle in the early 90's.

The collapse of the Japanese stock market and the Tokyo real estate market in 1993 and 1994.

The collapse of the emerging market economies throughout the world in the late 90's, including Thailand, Malaysia, Indonesia, Korea, Russia and Brazil.

The multi-billion dollar bankruptcy of Long Term Capital Management in 1998.

The collapse of the bubble in Internet stock valuations expected in the not too distant future.

Although each of these disastrous events had different immediate causes, they share a number of similar characteristics that leads me to believe that the free market, as structured today, may not be able to properly handle such events today or in the future. The shared characteristics are as follows:

Driven to Excess - Almost all of these debacles started with a very good idea, which typically was a big moneymaker early on. This initial success attracted a great number of other participants into the market to try to duplicate this success. What was once a unique idea became more commodity-like and unusually high profit margins were driven out of the business.

Other People's Money - Many of these investments were made by professional investors on behalf of their clients, using their clients' investment money, with the investment managers earning an annual fee and a percentage of the upside, with little to none of their own money at risk.

Use of Debt Leverage - Many of these investments utilized a significant amount of commercial bank debt or other debt leverage. As the amount of debt leverage increased, the investor's original equity contribution came to represent such a small percentage of the total investment funds that he began to act like an option holder, not an equity investor. Option holders, unlike true equity investors, seek very volatile situations because they benefit tremendously on the upside and yet on the downside their losses are limited to their original investment.

New Method of Valuation - Many of these bubbles persisted because people got wrapped up in a new methodology of valuation that often involved the greater fool theory. That is, people recognized that the valuations at which they were investing were extremely high, but they assumed that there would always be a greater fool who would take them out of their investments. This type of investing achieved notoriety when it was given its own name, momentum investing. Often these new types of investments create an historical track record that "proves" that the investment strategy yields spectacular results. The problem with these track records is that they are constructed during periods in which the economic event, which would be catastrophic to this type of investing, has not occurred. For example, all junk bonds do well during an economic expansion, but unfortunately, many get into trouble all together during a recession.

Group Dynamics - Often market participants begin to be more influenced by the actions and successes of other market participants than their own common sense. Short of mob psychology, this type of behavior, although irrational, can be understood when one imagines himself as a participant surrounded by others who are gaining enormous monetary benefit from following an investment policy that appears to be fundamentally flawed.

Lax Regulation and Poor Reporting Requirements - In most every case, the problem escalated because of poor government supervision or regulation. Problems that should have been reported in a timely manner were either not required to be disclosed or disclosure requirements were simply ignored.

Internet Mania

I happen to be one of the biggest proponents of the Internet. I believe it may be a more powerful invention than the television or the telephone. In general, Internet stocks deserve very aggressive valuations. They will, in many cases, end up being very successful companies. Even so, the valuations today far exceed rational expectations. The fact that the Internet will be successful does not guarantee that these particular Internet companies will be successful. There will be one or two Microsofts in the batch, but they will not all be Microsofts. If the current market valuation of all the Internet stocks that trade publicly today grew at 15% per year for 30 years, thus representing a fair and reasonable return to equity investors, the resulting companies would have a market value in 15 years greater than today's entire Fortune 500.

Many investors today know that the Internet marketplace is overvalued. That does not prevent them from investing. They not only hear stories about the enormous paper profits that their work associates have made in Internet stocks, they bear witness in the parking lot to the fancy new cars these work associates purchase with proceeds from Internet stock gains.

The valuation of Internet stocks is based on a new type of analysis that is not dependent on old-fashioned price-to-earnings ratios since most of these companies do not report positive earnings. Price-to-sales ratios and market value per hit seem to be the more popular valuation approaches. Unfortunately, it is profits and earnings that translate into cash flow that can be distributed to shareholders as a return on their investment. It is hard to dividend revenues or hits to investors.

Although the Internet will be of enormous value to consumers in the future, I doubt that great values will accrue to many Internet businesses. The reason is that unlike a brick and mortar business, there are few if no barriers to entry on the Internet. These newly emergent price discounters will be easy to find on the Internet as there will be Internet sites that specialize in sending out spiders that search the Internet for consumer bargains. This is great news for consumers but very bad news for Internet companies and their profits. My prediction is that Internet companies will grow very large and have very significant revenues, but will report very small profit margins and, therefore, never reward investors that are buying Internet stocks at the dramatic market values of today.

Anybody who buys an Internet stock today and believes he will recoup his investment as the company generates profits by selling advertising space on its site need only examine one valuation ratio today. The number of websites that are currently outstanding, approximately 40 million, creates so many opportunities and so much space for banner ads, that they may never generate significant revenue. Currently, 30 seconds of advertising on television during the Super Bowl costs approximately $1.5 million. For the same $1.5 million, an advertiser could purchase at today's market rates approximately 15 billion banner ads on the Internet. Clearly, advertising space on the Internet has a long way to go before catching up to its other media rivals and becoming a significant source of revenue to its virtual providers.

The Reforms Needed

The challenge is to implement reforms that motivate market participants to avoid these types of destructive behavior without implementing lots of unnecessary bureaucratic government regulation. For example, top executives at major U.S. companies today typically receive compensation between 5 to 50 times their salary in the form of options and warrants. These options clearly motivate managers to take risks and to seek growth, sometimes just for growth's sake. Because managers pay very little up-front monies for these options, they might be motivating executives to take unwarranted risks. A salaried manager is only acting as an agent on behalf of the owner. Options granted to management may get them thinking about the upside but may not motivate them to plan appropriately for the downside. Because most of the decisions in the world today are made by salaried employees rather than actual owners, we better be sure that their economic motivation systems agree with how we would like the economic world to develop.

These examples show that it is in everyone's interest to create a system in which all participants and their economic motivations are in line with society's view of how we wish to develop. Commercial bankers, investment fund managers, real-estate developers, investment bankers and others can do enormous damage if their personal motivations are structured so as not to benefit the economy in general. I fear the day when Robert Rubin, our Secretary of the Treasury, runs out of Band-Aids.

Our primary belief in this endeavor should be that America consists of our people, not our office buildings, factories or retail stores. To make America great, we must better our people. Increasing our industrial strength or expanding our global economic reach does nothing for America if it does not benefit our people. In suggesting possible solutions to our problems, we should highlight the un-American activities currently being sponsored by our U.S. corporations and U.S. commercial bankers and aided and abetted by a friendly Federal Reserve, unelected international trade bureaucrats, fat-cat U.S. Ambassadors, an acquiescing Export Import Bank and supported by a President and a U.S. Congress that have been bought and paid for with campaign contributions and lobbying perks. U.S. corporations are actively participating in a global economy in an attempt to exploit labor, including women and children and avoid many government regulations including consumer, labor, OSHA, product liability and environmental laws. These activities of U.S. corporations, their international subsidiaries and foreign companies controlled by them or substantially dependent on them for sales, have dramatic and negative consequences for many working Americans.

This type of activity by our major U.S. companies violates a basic social contract that Americans had historically with the companies located here. The American people have always been hard working and very proud of being American. In fact, many working Americans fought in one of five wars in the last 55 years to defend

America and what it stands for. Each working American contributes a portion of his hard-earned earnings to taxes that support the sick, the poor, the elderly and the unemployed in this country. And each of us not only obeys our country's laws but lives a life that honors the Constitution and our Declaration of Independence. We, as Americans, have an uplifting vision of the decency of all men and the human dignity they deserve. What our largest corporations and our government are doing to our hardest working citizens violates every oath of what it means to be an American.

At one time in our country's history it was deemed important to assure the separation of church and state. I think that the time has come for a separation of business and state. In 1941, there was a name for this marriage of business interests with the government. It was called fascism.

It is important to remember that free markets do create wealth. In our attempts to more equitably distribute this wealth, we must be sure not to kill the golden goose. We should not be afraid to introduce constraints on the free market, solely because we are afraid of disturbing its purity or theoretically perfect state.

I would suggest a number of changes to our current economic system. First, I would aggressively seek to break up monopoly power wherever it exists. I would also put a physical limit on the maximum size that our commercial banks and our largest corporations could grow to. These companies must be of a size that allows for fair competition, and more importantly, lets the worst performing companies seek bankruptcy and orderly liquidation without an overly burdensome cost to the society.

Commercial banks would have to be more closely regulated. Any losses would have to be recognized immediately. Problems in their loan portfolio would have to be disclosed openly. Any deterioration in their equity base or their ability to make loans would have to be disclosed immediately. Any failure to report any of this information would be held not only against the bank shareholders, but individually against each of its executives and directors. Bank regulators' accountability would be increased. Any attempts to unfairly influence bank regulators would be dealt with severely. Because, as we have seen, many of the problems associated with investment debacles and collapses involve a great deal of bank debt leverage, it is very important that we allow individual banks to fail if they do a poor job of supervising their lending activity. Banks should not encourage individuals and funds to leverage off other people's money and excessive bank debt in order to create option-like opportunities for themselves. Only if banks are allowed to fail by our government will their shareholders implement safeguards necessary to see that their lending programs are disciplined.

Banks currently have to be leveraged less than 20 to 1 in order to do business internationally. Given the significant amount of volatility in currency fluctuations, international capital flows and the amount of debt leverage on private enterprises, it might make sense to limit bank leverage to 10 to 1. Banks might have to charge an extra one percent per year on their loans in order to get an adequate return to their equity investors, but the ensuing stability of our economic system might be worth it.

One could imagine the immediate benefit of preventing our Federal Reserve from printing excess money and causing inflation. Because of many Keynesian economists' desire to maintain flexibility in the system, this is probably not practical. It does not seem excessive, however, to require that the Federal Reserve publish its intentions to print money and increase the money supply. Estimated amounts of new money, the percentage increases and estimates of general inflation could all be reported by the Federal Reserve on a timely basis.

To avoid another prolonged depression like 1929, the government should begin to develop a plan of action to stimulate the economy if it ever gets stuck at such a low economic output level again. Because government spending may be required to break the logjam and deficit spending should be avoided, maybe an emergency government fund should be created in anticipation of any future problem.

Chapter 2

Written in April 2003

Following are selected excerpts from *The Coming Crash in the Housing Market*

Following are selected excerpts from "The Coming Crash in the Housing Market", a book Talbott wrote and published in April 2003. The publisher was McGraw-Hill, Inc.

<u>Housing Prices Certainly Look Awfully High</u>

The first three rules of real estate are expressed as "location, location, location." Real estate is inherently a local business because the value of real estate directly correlates with regional economies and regional demographics. Specific metropolitan home real estate markets also have their own unique market characteristics, but the present chapter and most of the book look at the United States home real estate market in its entirety.

The reason for such a national analysis, which would seem to violate the above three rules of real estate, is that there are systemic problems in the way that home prices are determined and these systemic problems are national, if not international, in scope. Although each region of the country has its own unique issues with regard to its economic outlook and home valuations, the nation shares a common methodology for pricing and financing real estate. An inherent problem in the system could affect all areas of the country, albeit to varying degrees. In addition, mortgage interest rates are national, so if they are contributing to a possible overvaluation, the effect would be expected to hold nationwide.

Unless you dwell under a rather large rock, you probably already know that home prices in the United States have been increasing for some time now. The magnitude of the increase is indeed startling. Median housing prices for existing home sales in the United States increased eightfold over the past 35 years.

The Housing Market is Built on Leverage

We shall see that what makes an asset-based market like the home housing market risky is the sheer volume of the leverage or the debt in the system. Leverage is simply how much debt individuals and institutional players in the system carry against their assets. It is called leverage, or borrowing, because it leverages, or increases, the potential returns from an investment. A 5 percent return on an asset becomes a 50 percent return to equity capital if leveraged with nine dollars of debt for every one dollar of equity (ignoring for now the cost of the debt).

Because there is no free lunch in economics, the increased return potential is matched by an increased risk profile. The investor can easily turn any relatively safe asset like property into a risky investment by layering on debt. A rather safe income stream from the unleveraged asset can become a net income stream after interest expense that is much more volatile, unpredictable and risky.

Why would individuals wish to create such a risky asset? The answer is that the upside potential is enormous. If you had bought an average home in 1968 for the median average price of $20,000 available at the time and only put down $2,000, or 10 percent of the purchase price, your profit from selling in September 2002 would have been $140,000 (again for simplicity we ignore borrowing costs here, a reasonable assumption if you rent the property out and the rent covers the mortgage payments). This is a profit equal to 70 times your original $2,000 investment or 10 times what it would have been without the use of leverage.

So individuals should not be relied upon to limit their debt exposure, especially in highly leveraged financings like home mortgages, where the individual may view his investment as an option on higher real estate prices. Volatility and price appreciation are his friends as they both increase the value of his option and, therefore, the more leverage the better. Option theory predicts that buyers may try to buy the most expensive home possible, as this will give them control of the largest possible option contract.

If the individual is not motivated to control his debt leverage, then it must fall to the lenders to act as the debt police in such transactions. We will see that the lenders are also not very motivated to act as a damper on debt, either for the homeowner or for themselves.

The Leverage End Game: Foreclosure and Personal Bankruptcy

One of the most shocking statistics is the percentage of mortgages that enter into foreclosure proceedings each quarter. The total in foreclosure today is approximately 1.2 percent of the total mortgage debt outstanding, but this number is growing rapidly.

What is so shocking about it is not the upward slope of an ever-increasing rate of foreclosures. Foreclosures are not only increasing, but at an ever increasing rate. But this is not the real shock. The really shocking news is that foreclosures would be increasing at all, given that home prices are increasing in value at the fastest pace in history. One would naturally expect this curve to be not only flat, but declining. Just in the last three years the foreclosure rate has increased 25 percent, but we know that home prices increased 20 percent over these same three years. How can you have the foreclosure rate increasing while housing prices are increasing? Even if the homeowner loses his job or has other troubles in making his mortgage payments, in a strong housing market like this he can always sell his home at a profit and easily pay back the mortgage lender in full.

Here we see the foreclosure rate accelerating rather dramatically in the face of the healthiest and most robust housing market in history. What will happen if housing prices soften? What if people get in trouble through job losses, but do not have the option of selling their home quickly at a profit in order to repay the banks because home prices are down? We can tell you what will happen to the shape of this curve. It will no longer be a smooth upward sloping linear curve. There will be a big disconnect and the rate of foreclosures will jump enormously. This is one of the keys to our analysis in this book. Historical experience, especially in default rates and foreclosures, means next to nothing as those events occurred during a period of ever-increasing housing prices and a fairly healthy economy. If housing prices soften, then this type of historical experience is meaningless. And institutions such as banks, mortgage insurance providers, mortgage packagers, mortgage investors and others that are depending on an historical default rate continuing into the future are about to be rudely awakened.

On November 24, 2002, the *New York Times* reported that mortgage foreclosures were not just a bicoastal phenomenon. Nowhere is the problem of foreclosures worse than in Indiana, where the Mortgage Bankers Association of American found 2.22 percent of all housing in foreclosure, the highest rate in the country. Foreclosures are highest among so-called sub-prime loans, those higher-rate loans made to people with less than perfect credit ratings. "We're seeing the implications of reduced standards that sub-prime lenders applied. The expectations were that we would see more fail, and now we're seeing them fail," said William Apgar, the federal housing commissioner under Bill Clinton and now a senior scholar at the Joint Center for Housing Studies at Harvard.

As we said, 1.2 percent of all mortgages are currently in foreclosure. This is just part of the story. The number of personal bankruptcies has exploded over the last 20 years. Topping 1.5 million persons, homeowners make up more than half of this number. The number of homeowners claiming personal bankruptcy has jumped from 450,000 to over 750,000 in just five years. This has occurred as mortgage debt outstanding has jumped 50 percent to almost $5.7 trillion over the last four years.

The *Wall Street Journal* on November 13, 2002, quoted Elizabeth Warren, a Harvard law professor who specializes in consumer bankruptcy, as saying that there is a direct connection between the massive levels of mortgage-related debt and the rise in personal bankruptcies. "I think we're only seeing the front end of this wave," she said. The article reported that nearly one in five homeowners refinanced their mortgages in the past year, with 30 percent of those using some of the proceeds to pay down other debt. Professor Warren calls this an "unmitigated disaster" because it comes on top of ever-increasing amounts of credit card debt.

Not everyone is alarmed by the increasing trend in personal bankruptcies and mortgage foreclosures. Freddie Mac is the second largest purchaser and packager of mortgages and pass-through securities after Fannie Mae. Their chief economist, Frank Nothaft, says that he doesn't see the connection between the increase in personal bankruptcies and increased levels of mortgage borrowings. He blames increasing cultural acceptance of bankruptcy for the problem and thinks that refinancing that pledge people's homes as collateral to repay other debt is the right step for families to take to get out from under burdensome debt.

We will see that part of the problem here, as elsewhere, is that those institutions closest to this issue have the potential to let their narrow self-interest outweigh the public interest. Realtors, mortgage brokers, appraisers, commercial bankers, mortgage insurers, Fannie Mae and Freddie Mac, and even Alan Greenspan all have an interest in preserving confidence in the mortgage system, even if it is broke and in desperate need of fixing. Even Alan Greenspan? Yes, even Alan Greenspan. The reason is that he works for the Federal Reserve Board, which is owned and controlled by the country's commercial banks, which in turn hold plenty of home mortgage assets on their books. In addition, he has his hands full right now with a weak economy and a collapsing stock market. The last thing he needs right now is to have a housing crash. Remember, homeowners' spending of money that they have taken out of their homes through refinancing is one of the few bright spots of the current economy.

Perhaps you are aware of Washington's proposed solution to the increase in personal bankruptcies. Always willing to take the campaign money of the credit card and mortgage industries, Congress has concluded that the solution to the problem of too many bankruptcies is to make it much more difficult for citizens to claim bankruptcy. Specifically, people claiming bankruptcy would not free themselves of older debt obligations if they returned to a positive cash flow position in the near future. So much for giving someone a new start on life.

The fact is that this "solution" would do nothing to address the underlying cause of the problem. Banks and credit card companies are becoming more and more aggressive in their lending terms. Citibank, at one time in the 80's, rather than do credit analysis to determine if they take on a new credit card customer, decided to avoid most of the paperwork hassle and just mailed valid credit cards to millions of Americans around the country. Enormous bad debt losses resulted. We shall see that the aggressive terms of mortgage lenders is not only endangering the health of the mortgage market, but is also contributing to the unhealthy rise in home prices around the country and presenting a real threat to our country's economic prosperity.

Rational or Irrational Exuberance

Many believe that for a crash in a market to occur, the participants must have been behaving irrationally to begin with to allow prices to get so high. They draw little distinction between irrational participants and irrational markets. When a market appears overvalued, many leap to the conclusion that its participants are acting irrationally and they ignore the possibility that participants may actually be acting perfectly rationally, that is, while prices appear high relative to history, prices may indeed reflect people's beliefs that the economic good in question is going to be in greater and greater demand in the future and its supply will be limited, thus generating opportunities for increased earnings from the asset. Not all bubbles burst. Some continue to grow into successful companies or entire new industries. Just because prices are high relative to their historical levels does not mean that a bubble exists or that prices are sure to fall in the future.

In times of dramatically higher market prices, others are quick to declare that the market itself is acting irrationally. This is a serious charge to any market economist because it attacks the credibility of all markets. If free markets don't do the best job of assigning prices, then how can they do the best job of allocating resources? And if markets are subject to frequent bubbles and crashes, is a free market system the best system to organize an economy and a society around?

There is a very big difference between charging that some of the participants in a market are acting irrationally and concluding that the market itself is acting irrationally in setting prices. The best example of this occurs at horse racing tracks around the world. Anyone who has attended a horse race can tell you tales of the large number of railbirds at the track who are more than willing to share with you the secrets to their supposed success. Far from being rational, their "winning" strategies include betting on the color of the jockey's silks, the sound of the horse's name, the state where he was bred, the weight he is carrying or their favorite lucky number.

And, yet, out of this chaos, order comes. By the time the race starts, the odds on the tote board are a very good predictor of how the horses will run. Why is this? The reason is twofold. First, the true odds on the tote board are only affected by real bets, not chat along the rails. The odds follow the money. Second, if these odds get out of line with someone's best estimate of the correct odds, he or she can correct them by wagering money on the underpriced entry until the odds come into line and the arbitrage profit opportunity disappears. So here we have a very good example of many irrational participants and a very rational market.

Eugene Fama of the University of Chicago, my morning-line favorite to win the Nobel Prize in economics, has been a big defender of his path-breaking work on the efficiency of markets. Efficiency is another way of saying that market pricing acts rationally, that all available information is incorporated in the price and that the price is the best predictor of future opportunities. If markets are efficient, then bubbles should be rare, as prices should not be allowed to overinflate without someone, like the horse bettor at the track, stepping in and profiting from the error and returning the price to normal. Prices can appear relatively high, but it should be impossible to predict in advance whether they will continue ever upward, or will turn and head south. Market efficiency at its simplest says it is impossible to beat the market over the long term.

If these behaviorists are right about their theories of mispricing about the market, it should create money-making opportunities for either them or their clients. They should be able to start mutual funds that make trades based on their theories of the market's mispricing, buying underpriced assets and selling overpriced ones. If they are right about their behaviorist theories, their mutual funds should be exceptionally good long-term performers, dramatically outperforming the market indexes. Unfortunately, no such mutual fund exists in real life.

So what am I doing writing this book? Market theory predicts that the current high home prices are a good predictor of future home price performance and we know that real markets are less susceptible to bubbles and crashes because of efficient pricing and that because some participants are irrational does not make the entire market pricing system irrational or inefficient. But I hold the opposite view. I believe that current home prices are artificially high and due for a major correction downward. And I don't think the reason is because the market participants are irrational. As a matter of fact, I believe that the homeowners and lenders and guarantors are doing exactly what you or I would do in a similar situation -- namely, they are each acting very rationally. So how can I conclude that the market is overvalued? The answer is that the housing market in the United States is not a true "market" at all.

Economists mean something very specific when they talk about "free markets," and there are a number of very important underlying assumptions that must be met before transactions or exchanges can be characterized as belonging to a market, with its guarantees of efficiency and rational pricing.

We all remember from Economics 101 that the exchanges in a free market must be first of all voluntary and non-coercive. In the case of our housing market this appears to be satisfied as no one is forcing us to take out a mortgage or buy a house (spouses don't count). Second, the exchanges must be at arm's length. We will reexamine this assumption when we talk about real estate appraisers and their close incestual relationship to mortgage bankers later in this chapter. Third, the benefits and costs of the transaction must accrue fully to the price negotiators. To the extent that there are costs that might fall upon third parties not represented during the negotiated pricing, such as

U.S. taxpayers if the U.S. government is providing debt guarantees, we may have a serious problem with the pricing mechanism for homes and mortgages.

Finally, and most important for my argument that homes are overpriced in today's market is the requirement that a market have many willing participants, that is, numerous buyers and sellers. Although there are a large number of willing buyers and sellers in the housing marketplace in the form of homeowners, it is my contention that their actions are controlled by a very few number of very large lending institutions. In a world where most of the buyers are leveraged over 80 percent with mortgage debt, I argue that the mortgage lender and his lending terms are the key ingredients to setting home prices in America. We will see that because of competition between these very few lenders, they end up with very aggressive lending policies, which drive up housing prices with little real recourse to the lending institutions. Finally, we will explore the impact that an implied government guarantee has on the operations of Fannie Mae and Freddie Mac, those unfortunate private companies that must compete with them, and the overall mortgage and housing industries.

If indeed the housing market is not a real economic market, this has very serious ramifications. Most important, participants cannot assume that prices are rational. They cannot assume that bubbles will not occur. In a market system, individual participants need not do a lot of investigatory work with regard to the reasonableness of prices because they know it is a market and by definition the prices have to be reasonable. Going back to the racetrack analogy, the guy picking horses based on the color of the silks has just as good a chance of winning as the Ph.D. in statistics sitting next to him. The reason is that the final odds, or the price of each horse's chances of winning, reflect all available information, even all of the Ph.D.'s hard statistical work. The railbird is able to get a "free ride" on the hard statistical work of others and is given the same odds or pricing as the Ph.D. for every horse in the race.

But if the housing market is not a pure market, are homebuyers making a mistake when they assume that the price they are paying is a market price so it must, de facto, be fair? Most of their investigative work before buying is to determine the market price of other homes in the neighborhood, but if this is not a true market what good is this "market" information? This should scare most homebuyers as almost all information they have about a home's value comes from appraisals based completely on the prices of similar properties sold recently in the "market."

What's Wrong with Leverage?

Many homeowners are very highly leveraged. Many have purchased homes in the last three years with maximum amounts of debt, and many have refinanced their homes as rates have declined. Unfortunately, many of these refinancings involved re-leveraging the property back up to 80 or 90 percent loan-to-value ratios. In addition to paying off the old high-cost mortgage, many who refinanced took it as an opportunity to repay credit card balances, student loans, auto and boat loans, or to make general improvements on their home. If there was borrowing capacity left over, homeowners ended up buying bigger cars and faster boats. Besides the high amount of debt on their homes, there are a couple of additional problems with these transactions.

First, encouraged by tax laws that make mortgage interest deductible, the homeowner was motivated to consolidate his unsecured debts and give up a security interest in his home to his previously unsecured creditors. Now, if he has trouble paying what was his credit card balance, his home is at risk.

Second, in Hollywood there is an expression that the budget for a picture is "up on the screen." What they mean is that all the monies contributed to the making of the movie went into direct costs for the picture -- actors, director, script, producer, costumes, scenery, etc. There was no leakage of funds to other non-picture-related ventures. This is important because a lender to the picture wants to know that his asset, the picture, is composed of all the budget monies spent to date. It is his only assurance that monies contributed actually went to improving the quality of the asset. This is important in any secured-type lending because if there is a problem, selling the asset is the only recourse a creditor has in trying to recoup his investment.

With home refinancing, there is no such guarantee. Lenders can extend monies, and debt can be attached to the property, but the funds can be appropriated for numerous and varied purposes other than improving the quality of the home. When one borrows against his or her home and uses the money to buy a car or repay credit card debt, the money is definitely not "up on the screen." The housing asset's quality has not improved, but the debt attached to the property has grown dramatically. In any secured lending business, this is a recipe for disaster.

The dramatic amount of leverage utilized by the homebuyer also can contribute to a scenario in which home prices are overvalued. Because home purchasers are often required to only put 1 to 10 percent of the total purchase price down in cash, they in effect are playing with other people's money. Milton Friedman has posited that we manage our own money best, and that if we are asked to buy something with other people's money, the ensuing mess is only surpassed by a situation in which we are asked to buy something for someone else with someone else's money.

Once a homeowner leaps in logic to realizing he is playing with other people's money, his entire motivation changes. Now he can think of himself as an option holder where for a small amount of money he can control the upside of a very large and expensive piece of real estate. If worse comes to worse, he can always walk away, leaving the property to the bank and work his way through the bankruptcy court. This is a very rational approach to wealth maximization. If the average American has a net worth of $70,000, mostly in his home and banks are willing to lend him $300,000 to buy a beautiful new home, his downside is the $15,000 required down payment plus as much of the $55,000 of his remaining net worth the bank can get their hands on. The upside is a home that might double in value every five years, if historical trends hold. Option theory says that such an individual, far from avoiding risk, will seek out highly volatile pricing situations that maximize the value of his option. More importantly, if given the chance to own a small home or a large expensive home, such an option investor will always choose the biggest property with the most leverage. So much for the concept of the homeowner controlling his pricing behavior. And yet no economist would accuse him of acting irrationally. Looking at the home purchase as an option contract means that the homeowner is encouraged to take greater risks, buy bigger properties and utilize the maximum amount of leverage.

Do Banks and Appraisers Act Rationally?

Surely, large commercial banks will be motivated to act rationally in this process. If the banks make stupid loans, these loans will eventually come back to haunt them in higher default rates, lower corporate earnings, reduced share prices, lowered debt ratings and higher long-term borrowing costs -- at least that is what my economics textbook says.

Unfortunately, we have seen time and time again that the internal organizations of very large financial institutions are not necessarily geared to reflect market and economic reality. First, individuals at the bank make lending decisions, and not the corporate institution itself. Business organizations try very hard to align the interests of their individual employees with the corporation's goals and objectives, but in a very large institution this is incredibly difficult, if not impossible. Individuals can be motivated by hefty bonuses to bring in mortgage loan business and maximize fee income, but it is very difficult to punish them for defaults, especially if they occur much later after the loans were booked, or occur all at the same time due to some systemic problems in the system. Thus employees also act like option holders in that they are much more concerned with the potential upside of a transaction than its downside. I mean you can only get fired once, but the upside of success is limitless. I have never known of a company employee who had to pay his company if he erred and the firm lost money. To the extent that managers of the bank are indeed real common stock option holders in their company, this only exacerbates this option upside and couples it with a limited downside mentality.

The large fees attached to mortgage loans and the attractive profit spreads between the mortgage yields and the banks' cost of funds means that the banks and their employees will be very motivated to add mortgage loans aggressively to their portfolio. Well maybe not make them a permanent addition to their portfolio, but to book them aggressively.

There is a second fundamental economic problem in industries such as mortgage banking, insurance or airlines that deal with long-term assets and liabilities. Because traumatic-type events only occur once in a great while, the managers are motivated to offer noneconomic terms in order to generate business. This leads to tougher and tougher price competition followed by very regular industry shakeouts. In the mortgage business this means you have to offer incredibly aggressive terms with regard to total amounts of lending, rates, degree of leverage allowed, etc., or your competitor will, and you will lose a customer. This almost ensures that home prices will be overinflated eventually.

Banks have another important reason not to worry a great deal about the credit quality of their mortgage lending, 75 percent of the mortgage loans they originate get sold and never appear on their balance sheet. Most are sold to Fannie Mae or Freddie Mac who act as buyers of mortgages, such that the bank never has to feel any pain if transactions were done at too high a price or with too much debt and end up in default or foreclosure. With this as the end game, there is no reason for the bank to worry about what price homes achieve. It is not going to be their worry. We will see in the end who ought to worry. (Look to your left, look to your right, all three of you may turn out to be suckers.)

Another reason to be concerned about a possible housing crash has to do with how appraisals in the housing industry are done. Typically, when you do an appraisal of an asset or business you look at what the asset's value might be under many different markets or scenarios. For example, if you are appraising a small business, you would want to know what its market value had been historically, what it might garner if sold today in the merger market, the price you could get if you took it public in the stock market, the proceeds realized if you had to quickly liquidate it and sell its hard property and equipment in the real estate and real property markets, and even what price the management could pay if they borrowed and bought the business as a leveraged buyout.

It turns out that home real estate appraisals are much less thorough. It is the nature of most home properties that they aren't really good for much other than as a home. That means that their sole value is in the housing market. It is hard to imagine selling a home in order that it be converted to a church, school or office.

As we have seen, given the dramatic increase in the price of homes, appraisers put little weight on historical pricing. All they care about is indicators of current market pricing -- the best indicator of which is what other similar homes have sold for recently in the neighborhood. To the extent that other recent sales might be overpriced due to some of the systemic problems raised here, this assures that the appraisal will be overpriced. As if this were not enough of a self-fulfilling feedback loop, Fannie Mae increases the maximum amount that they will lend in a conventional mortgage each year by indexing it to, you guessed it, an index of home prices. As home prices increase, Fannie Mae is authorized to lend more in each conventional mortgage, and as Fannie Mae lends more, housing prices increase. Which do you think comes first, the chicken or the egg? Everything in the system -- pricing, financing, buyouts and appraisals -- are all tied together and racing forward in a fast and furious dance. Where will you be when the clock at the ball strikes 12 and where will your dance partners be?

The problem is worsened, if that could be possible, by questionable practices on behalf of mortgage brokers and appraisers. It is common knowledge that the first piece of news an appraiser hears after getting a new business call from a mortgage banker is the dollar amount of the appraisal necessary to justify the amount of borrowing the homeowner needs to do. If you want to borrow $240,000, you better have a $300,000 house, and I know just the appraiser to make sure that you do. It reminds me of the story of the guy who said his dog was worth $10,000. When challenged by his friend on how he was so sure he had a $10,000 dog, the dog owner replied, "Well, he better be. I just traded two $5,000 cats for him."

So what is this rational argument that home prices are due for a major crash in the very near future? First of all, I don't pretend to be able to foretell the future, so I cannot predict exactly which quarter the crash is likely to occur. I can say that the longer it is delayed, and the higher we allow prices to go, the more severe it will be. The problem is that prices are abnormally high. The fact that they will adjust downward in a crash is the solution, not the problem. The reason we call it a crash is that even if it is as small as a 10 to 20 percent adjustment downward, due to the leverage of individual homeowners, this is sufficient to cause major problems for a great number of families. A move of this magnitude could wipe out the entire equity that many families have in their homes, force some into foreclosure, possibly threaten many families' entire net worth, and act as a detriment to the health of the general economy, as many people will be prevented from selling their homes if the debt balances exceed the market value of their homes.

In the end, what is it that gives us the greatest cause for concern when we look at the precarious heights that home prices have attained? Is it the somewhat crazy irrational behavior of buyers caught up in feeding frenzy? Is it the fact that the housing market, on close inspection, doesn't look like a free market at all? Is it that buyers and lenders are acting more like option holders than prudent property investors and creditors? Is it that the assets are being passed around so fast that it is hard to find the institution ultimately responsible? Or is it simply that a government guarantee has assured irrationality as participants take on greater and greater risk for less and less real profit?

It is all these things. And one more: Through the mechanizations of the modern sophisticated mortgage market, not only has liquidity increased dramatically, all sense of self-policing has disappeared. By dramatically increasing the diversification of holders of mortgage securities, and by getting an implied guarantee from the federal government, arrangers have distilled the impact of defaults to the point that no one seems concerned or involved. As I have seen in my work with poor developing countries that lack democracy, such a lack of a self-policing mechanism is a recipe for disaster. The free markets operate efficiently because smart investors win and bad investors lose. The housing market has been built where everyone seems to win, something that Adam Smith will not allow to continue forever.

Homeowners Have Been Lulled to Sleep

Homeowners have grown accustomed to a world of aggressive mortgage brokers, realtors and bankers. It is hard to imagine a future world in which 'For Sale" signs stand on lawns for years rather than days, where instead of multiple offers above the asking price, you are faced with taking numerous discounts to your asking price, where you need to serve lunch at your open house just to get the brokers to come over and look, and where banks have retrenched with new lending policies that include asking questions like what did this property sell for 10 years ago. If bankers retrench, and we assure you that is what they do for a living (just ask any farmer in the Midwest), then all the formulas you know for lending and pricing go out the window. There will be no comparables in the neighborhood because nothing will be selling. Bankers will have to go back to very realistic valuations, probably based on square footage and historical pricing. Valuations will further be damaged by the banks' own activity as they dump foreclosed properties on the market at huge discounts to the mortgage amount. Banks really do not want to hold bad loans on their books because it only reminds them of managerial errors of the past. They are infamous for buying high and selling low when it comes to foreclosures. Unfortunately, their aggressive selling will only exacerbate an already weak property market.

To homeowners this means that whatever rosy assumptions they had about refinancing, taking money out in the form of a second mortgage equity loan, or selling at a high price to a buyer financed by aggressive bank formulas will all basically evaporate at the same time. When an entire market's sense of value is based solely on current "market" values, then be prepared for a wild ride when those market prices come under attack from a less aggressive banking sector.

Bankers and Regulators Have Also Been Lulled to Sleep

It is not only the homeowner who has been comforted by a constantly increasing market for home prices. The supposed experts -- realtors, appraisers, mortgage bankers, commercial bankers, and even Fannie Mae and Freddie Mac -- are all showing signs of dozing off. It is true that lending institutions and mortgage investors take great care to limit their exposure to interest rate and early principal repayment risks in their portfolios. There is much less they can do to limit their exposure to default risk in their mortgage portfolio.

The two traditional methods for limiting exposure to default risk in a housing mortgage portfolio are to limit the amount of each loan relative to the property's market value and to diversify geographically. Because of competitive pressures it is very difficult to run a conservative bank in the mortgage lending business and only work with big down-payment customers. If you don't do a no-points, low-fee, 97 percent loan-to-value mortgage, the guy down the street certainly will.

As far as diversifying geographically, this has been an excellent strategy to date because most of our country's housing problems historically have had an epicenter to them: the Internet bust hit Seattle and San Jose, the oil glut hit Houston and Dallas and Wall Street's corruption scandal will most likely hit New York worst of all. But what if the next problem were national in scope? To the extent that there is a systemic problem with the way the entire mortgage industry extends credit, then geographic diversification is much less effective in stemming default losses.

Even the AAA-rated behemoths of the mortgage business, Fannie Mae and Freddie Mac, are not without risk. We shall see that they have added incredible amounts of leverage to their businesses. How they got their triple-A rating might have more to do with the financial health of the U.S. taxpayer than with either institution's credit quality, as they lean heavily on their implied government guarantee. Many of their most highly leveraged mortgages depend on private mortgage insurance (PMI) providers for risk management and these providers themselves are beginning to feel a bit of a pinch. It would only seem prudent to ask the question: What would have to happen before these PMI providers themselves were at risk?

Again, Fannie Mae and Freddie Mac have gained comfort by utilizing the most sophisticated forms of interest rate hedging and maturity matching. But, given the degree of leveraging throughout the system, they have probably not done as adequate a job as they should in analyzing how they would fare in a real housing price downturn with a significant number of foreclosures.

How Will it Begin?

We are living in an unusual time. It is the best of times and it is the worst of times. Many Americans are enjoying a standard of living unattainable by many on the planet. There is still substantial poverty in the country and incomes seem to be bifurcating, but we have enjoyed a dramatic increase in prosperity over the last 20 years. People are working hard and as we have seen, in many families both parents must work in order to pay the mortgage.

Storm Warnings

But there are storm warnings on the horizon. Government, having gotten too cozy with business, has resulted in lax accounting oversight and weakened business regulation that has damaged investors' confidence in the market. Interest rates are at 40-year lows, and yet there is little pickup in business activity. With short rates near 1 percent, the tried-and-true formula for stimulating the economy by just cutting interest rates is beginning to make less and less sense. Similarly, the rule of cutting taxes to stimulate the economy is harder to follow in a world of trillion-dollar deficits. Huge windfalls have already been generated for the wealthiest in the form of reduced income taxes, capital gains tax cuts, inheritance tax cuts and the government's having made it easier for U.S. businesses to relocate off shore and avoid all taxes.

The world is looking to the U.S. market as the driving consumer force supporting enormous worldwide production. Japan still is not growing, due mostly to the inability of its government to deal with bad loan problems at its largest banks. Japan is the classic example of what can go wrong when government gets too close to business. At one time admired for finding a new paradigm of business and government cooperation, Japan's system has now been exposed for what it is, corrupt cronyism. Europe is doing well, but has its hands full in incorporating the eastern European countries into the European Community, with the eventual planned admittance of Turkey and Russia expected soon thereafter.

Although we cannot predict the future and have always avoided the opportunity to guess interest rates or stock market movements, the future's impact on the housing market can be determined without any prior fortune-telling experience. The reason is quite simple. I will show that regardless of whether interest rates increase or decrease in the future, it will be bad for housing prices. If rates increase, it will be a sign of increased business activity, or it may signal a return of inflation if our government stupidly starts printing money to fund our deficits. Either way, we would expect housing prices to suffer if rates increase. The reason is that new homebuyers would qualify for significantly lower sums of home financing, even if their incomes remained the same. A small increase in wages of say 3 to 5 percent from a stronger economy would be dwarfed in the lenders' qualifying formula if rates increased from 6 to 8 percent (a 25 percent increase in rate levels from the formula's perspective).

If rates decrease in the future, things also look quite bleak for housing. While the qualifying formula will justify higher and higher amounts of leverage, we would expect foreclosures and bankruptcies to explode. The reason is that if long Treasury rates drop below 3 percent, there is a high likelihood of a deflationary spiral, a danger we have not faced in this country since the Great Depression. Supposedly, we learned our lesson during that depression that we should not tighten money supply in a recession, but given the current policies of an always inflation-fighting Fed, that might be exactly what they end up doing. If it happens, it will send our economists scrambling for their college textbooks as not one has dealt with deflation in generations and no one has a good idea as to how to handle it.

So you might ask what does this all mean to me? I am a homeowner, but I locked in my mortgage rate for 30 years and I'm not planning on selling any time soon. So what if a rate increase slows new home buying, bankrupts some ARM borrowers or depresses home prices? Well, the answer is that the depressed home prices could have a very real effect on the economy.

First, there is a wealth effect on consumption. When people feel wealthier, either from increases in their stock portfolio or from increases in the values of their homes, they tend to spend more. This has very real effects on the health of an economy. Economists have found that people spend more of each dollar of appreciation in their homes than in their stock portfolios because they seem to view the price increase as more permanent, because their homes are much more leveraged and because there are many available methods to borrow against increased home prices, including second mortgages and home equity loans. *Fortune* magazine on October 28, 2002, reported that economists John Quigley of Berkeley, Robert Shiller of Yale and Karl Case of Wellesley showed that for every $1,000 a house appreciates, homeowners spend $60 or 0.6 percent. This compares with 0.3 percent for stock market increases.

Fortune also reported that in 2001 and 2002, homeowners took $350 billion in cash out of their houses through refinancing and home equity loans. (In November of 2002, *USA Today* reported that economy.com expected the total to be closer to $420 billion for the two years combined.) So far they have spent some $70 billion on consumption goods that has helped to prop up the economy in a recession. The Federal Reserve estimates that they will use $120 billion to pay down credit card and other consumer debt. That leaves $165 billion still unspent. Not only would this consumption activity stop if home prices fell, but it would reverse itself as homeowners would have to consume less in order to feel comfortable with their reduced housing net worth.

Second, if home prices fall, it could have a very real effect directly on the economy. The reason is that if a significant percentage of homeowners find themselves living in an underwater asset, then labor mobility could be disrupted. As we said earlier, an asset is considered underwater when its total debts exceed its market value. This shouldn't make a difference to the long-term holder, but it becomes a real problem for someone wishing to sell his home in order to take a new job in a new town or someone who must sell to face a financial crisis such as job loss, medical problems or divorce. The inability of people to sell their homes easily to take on better job opportunities has a dramatic impact on labor mobility. Labor mobility is something we have come to take for granted in our economy, but without it an economy suffers terribly. Real growth is almost impossible without labor mobility. Job shuffling is the physical manifestation of the economic principle of employing all labor resources at their most efficient allocation. If labor mobility suffers, recessions are likely to be prolonged.

How Bad Can It Get?

We have seen that in a healthy economy with ever-increasing home prices, 1.2 percent of mortgages have entered foreclosure; therefore, it would not seem unrealistic to see foreclosures of 5 percent if the economy heads lower and home prices decline. Remember, foreclosures are much more likely when prices decline because the alternative of selling at a profit and repaying the debt in full is taken off the table. This means an additional three million family homes may enter foreclosure with a total potential property loss of $100 billion. This could have devastating effects on the upstream holders and guarantors of residential mortgage debt in this country and on the country as a whole.

The big change in the marketplace over the last 25 years has been the growth of the pass-through market. Mortgage pass-throughs provide incredible liquidity to a very long-term asset. Bankers are able to focus on origination without tying up their long-term capital. In essence, they package the mortgages and sell them to an institution more likely to want to invest for the long term, namely pension funds and life insurance companies. Traditionally invested in straight coupon bonds, these institutions insist that they not suffer high prepayment risk from the mortgages and that they have adequate guarantees or insurance against default. Mortgage insurance companies and mortgage packagers like Fannie Mae and Freddie Mac step in to play these roles.

For all the commercial banks in the country, the total mortgages on their books equaled $1.5 trillion at the end of 1999. In addition, the banks hold an additional $100 billion in home equity loans, which are much riskier loans than first-mortgage loans. Home mortgage debt alone dwarfs the banks' total equity, ignoring all the other types of loans on the banks' books. If the banks lost 30 percent of the value of all their residential mortgage holdings, it would wipe out the combined book equity of all the banks in the country. Now, we agree such a scenario is extremely unlikely, but the envisioned result is rather disturbing. For example, it they only lost 3 percent of their mortgage portfolio value, their equity accounts would take a 10 percent hit.

So what are the risks that our banks could have a problem in their mortgage debt portfolios? Banks are experiencing higher and higher foreclosure rates, even during the healthiest housing market in history. Banks have written off billions of bad loans in their overall lending portfolios in the last 20 years. Banks have maintained their profitability by continuing to increase fees to their customers. Fees on ATM transactions are very popular, at least with bankers, with many banks charging their own customers double fees if they use some other bank's ATM machine. But fees in general have exploded with some banks charging you to talk to a teller, some charging $105 to bounce three $2 checks and many charging lots of bizarre document and other esoteric fees to close a mortgage. Without this fee income, the banks' poor lending record would have driven their stock prices down substantially.

The Role of Private Mortgage Insurance Providers

Banks, however, are not the institutions at greatest risk if there is a crash in housing prices. That honor goes to the smaller private mortgage insurance providers. Private mortgage insurance (PMI) providers are those insurance companies that guarantee investors that interest and principal will be paid in the event of a mortgage foreclosure or default. The PMI industry acts as a linchpin guaranteeing the safety of highly leveraged home mortgages as investments.

Over $750 billion of mortgages outstanding are covered by private mortgage insurance. These are the riskiest of mortgages because the homeowner typically puts less than 20 percent down at time of purchase, thus necessitating the need for private insurance. And, yet, only two PMI companies are of a size to withstand any sizeable losses -- AIG and GE Credit -- and they control only approximately 30 percent of the total market for PMI.

The vast majority of the players in PMI are less than AAA-rated and are relatively small players in relation to the size of the risks they are underwriting. Five companies control a 70 percent market share, have insured mortgages totaling in excess of $530 billion and yet have combined shareholder equity of only $11 billion. They are MGIC Corp., The PMI Group, Inc., Radian Group, Republic Insurance and Triad Guaranty. How can five insurance companies with total equity of $11 billion survive if their $530 billion of residential mortgage debt starts to default? The simple answer is that they will not.

Not only is the PMI industry at greatest risk if there is a downturn in home prices, they are also the most critical element in the entire home mortgage business. If the PMI industry gets in trouble, mortgage investors get in trouble, liquidity evaporates for home mortgages, rates shoot up, qualifying formulas for new homebuyers tighten and home prices decline. So the feedback to the marketplace from a minor price decline might indeed be a more major decline.

Fannie Mae and Freddie Mac -- A Potential $3 Trillion Problem?

If a contagion reaches inside the comfortable offices of Fannie Mae and Freddie Mac, there is no pessimistic scenario I can describe that will adequately depict the ensuing disaster.

Many who examine these two very large companies are initially swayed into complacency by their sheer size, their AAA ratings and their incredible record of reported earnings growth over the years. The GSEs (Government Sponsored Entities, namely Fannie and Freddie) accomplished this dominant size with very little real equity. Counting all their mortgage debt holdings and guarantees, Freddie Mac is levered 71 times its equity of $17.6 billion and Fannie Mae is levered 116 times its equity of $15 billion. The Basel Accord of 1988 maintains that international banks have to maintain maximum leverage ratios of 12 to 1 on their loan portfolios and 24 to 1 on their residential mortgage portfolios. Unfortunately, the GSEs do not need to comply with Basel. These GSEs are incredibly large institutions, two of the largest financial institutions in the world, which also happen to have possibly the highest leverage in the world.

In my opinion, companies as leveraged as these two behemoths, narrowly focused in just one business and one asset class, do not deserve a triple-A rating. Their rating reflects neither their financial performance nor their financial condition, but something much more basic: their corporate charters. Both were "privatized" in the 1970s and 1980s when they were spun off from the federal government. Rather than becoming fully private enterprises, they maintained some very important advantages of being quasi-public agencies of the federal government. But the big daddy of perks is more implied than clearly stated. The marketplace clearly believes that the federal government stands behind and guarantees all Fannie Mae and Freddie Mac debt and commitments. It is because of this implied U.S. government guarantee that the GSEs have triple-A ratings and can borrow at almost the same rate as the federal government.

This low borrowing cost is an enormous subsidy provided by American taxpayers and is estimated at $4.5 billion per year by the Congressional Budget Office. If this subsidy just went toward lower mortgage rates no one would be the worse.

The problems with giving your largest industry participants a government guarantee is multifaceted. First, it puts other private competitors at an enormous disadvantage. This means that the GSEs can fund their mortgage costs at such low government guaranteed rates that they can buy business at yields that make no sense for private businesses. You would expect industry consolidation in the hands of the GSEs and that is just what has happened, with approximately 90 percent of all conventional mortgages being held or guaranteed by the GSEs. Not only is such consolidation bad for any industry, but also the implied government guarantee of the GSEs allows them to do many noneconomic things to win business.

Second, the government guarantee allows the GSEs to be much more aggressive financially and not pay any financial cost for their irresponsible actions in terms of higher borrowing costs. Every day companies make decisions as to how aggressive they will be in how they finance their business, but they know there will be a cost: the more inexpensive debt they use in their capital structure relative to expensive equity, the higher yield they will have to pay debt investors to purchase that debt. For the GSEs, there is no such trade-off between increased risk and financing costs. No matter how badly they run their business, their financing costs do not change, thanks to the federal government's implied guarantee.

Now it also turns out that the GSEs are very much like private companies in one very important aspect: They grant their managers and executives enormous stock option plans. So like good private businessmen they are motivated to improve earnings and increase their stock prices. But unlike a normal management team, and because of their government guarantee, they can do some fairly risky things to try to create shareholder value. The only thing I can think of that is worse than having a government agency as a competitor is to have a for-profit business as a competitor that has a government guarantee.

The prime example of how the GSEs increase profitability by increasing risk is by increasing leverage. Increased leverage always increases the rate at which earnings grow, but it also increases the rate at which earnings decline in bad times and raises breakevens. The extra debt should increase the firm's borrowing costs, but thanks to the federal guarantee this doesn't happen for the GSEs. When the GSEs increased debt leverage in their business, they did it solely to enhance the value of their employee stock options. They didn't care a hoot that they were endangering the entire mortgage market of the United States. Running a government business for private gain reminds me of Ross Perot's attempt to privatize the post office in which all he asked for in return was 10 percent of the savings.

Second, when the GSEs ran out of conventional mortgages to buy, they started going after sub-prime mortgages. "These are multifamily and second mortgages or lower credit first mortgages that carry a great deal more risk than conventional mortgages. But, no worries, mate -- the GSEs' borrowing rates will not change thanks to the government guarantees."

Finally, and probably most offensively, to add assets as fast as possible, the GSEs didn't go out and find new homebuyers that wanted to secure a mortgage -- they simply went out in the secondary market and bought a bunch of mortgages off the street. No productive activity here, just a chance to pop earnings by living off their low government guaranteed borrowing rate. Buying secondary assets on the street is in direct violation of the GSEs' charters that call for them to supply mortgage money to homebuyers.

Oh, I forgot: Where Fannie Mae and Freddie Mac used to book only about 25 percent of their total commitments and just guarantee the rest for others to hold, now they book approximately 60 percent, leaving few mortgages for anyone else to hold. The reason is simple: If they take the increased risks of interest rate risk, early principal repayment risk and counterparty risk inherent in holding a mortgage rather than just guaranteeing it, their profit margins increase nearly fourfold. Oh, yes, and once more their borrowing costs do not change to reflect the riskier strategy because of their government guarantee.

The Next Great Disaster

I am at a loss when I try to compare the GSEs to anything I have seen previously. Given their lack of regulation, the enormous utilization of derivatives in their business and the general complexity of their financial statements, they share characteristics of other troubled companies of late. I challenge anybody to read their annual reports and tell me within $3 billion how much real cash flow either of them makes each year.

If things turn badly, this situation might have the potential to be similar to the S&L collapse of the 1980s. Like the S&Ls, they hold only home mortgages, an asset that nobody has ever figured out a way to make riskless or to fix maturity on without a government guarantee. Also, like the S&Ls, they enjoy an enormous government guarantee and subsidy in their borrowing costs. Finally, they both suffered through stressful times, the S&Ls during the high interest rates of the eighties and the GSEs in their self-imposed prison of trying to provide constantly increasing profits for Wall Street, their stock price and their management options. If home prices decline, that just might be the straw that breaks the GSEs' backs.

An examination of Fannie Mae and Freddie Mac's most recent annual and quarterly reports raises serious questions as to what the effects of all this risk-taking has been on the cash flow available to shareholders. I cannot emphasize enough how convoluted Fannie

Mae's financial reports are, so I raise these concerns only as questions, to which Fannie Mae's management will hopefully have some good answers.

Over the last two years, Fannie Mae seems to have earned $28 billion in after-tax cash flow, paid $2.5 billion in dividends, but had their book equity remain flat. What did they do with the money? I first thought that they had accomplished major share repurchases. I checked and they had repurchased $2.0 billion worth of shares during this period, but their total shares outstanding barely changed. In essence, for every share they repurchased, they issued an option share to management. Too bad Fannie Mae is not subject to regulation by the Securities and Exchange Commission.

The biggest problem driving the apparently irrational behavior of the GSEs' managements is the implied guarantee of the federal government for its liabilities. We have seen that this guarantee not only drives the GSEs to do riskier and riskier things to increase profits but also has had an overreaching impact on the entire mortgage industry. Competitors, as well as suppliers to the GSEs, have to take greater and greater business risk at smaller and smaller margins if they wish to compete or do business with the GSEs. It is generally impossible to have a stable market when one of the competitors has no incentive to control its risk-taking.

Even without the government guarantee issue, industries with long asset lives such as the airlines, the banks, the insurance business and the mortgage business have long had a reputation for behavior that we will characterize as "irrational competitiveness." It is the nature of industries with very long assets and liabilities and very small probabilities of tragic events, that the participants will compete on price until they no longer adequately allow for all hard-to-define risks in their pricing. In the short term, business flows to the competitor who ignores the long-term risks and therefore prices his services too low. In a competitive market, there is great pressure on the other participants to match this mispricing. If they do not, they will not have any customers. Of course, we have seen the result of such cyclic behavior. Profits and retained earnings are driven to such a low level that when the tragic scenario occurs, many of the market participants do not have adequate equity cushions to withstand them. Some view such industry shakeouts as healthy, and compared to government bailouts, we would have to agree. But it seems as if the dislocations to customers, employees and taxpayers might be avoided if we could do a better job identifying the industries subject to this type of behavior and isolate its effects. The mortgage industry is exactly such a long-lived asset industry. Irrational competitors will drive rational players out of the market, will crush profit margins in good times and will not survive the bad times ahead.

What You Can Do About It

Action Item 1:
Decrease Your Exposure to Residential Real Estate

Action Item 2:
Move from a High-Priced Area to a Lower-Priced Area

Action Item 3:
Manage Your Debt Leverage Better

Action Item 4:
Hedge Your Exposure to Residential Real Estate

Action Item 5:
Plan Now in Case of a Major Transition Event

Action Item 6:
Examine Other Contingency Plans

Action Item 7:
Maintain Adequate Insurance

Action Item 8:
Investigate Bankruptcy Protections Now

Action Item 9:
Become More Civically Involved

Action Item 10:
Reassess Your Life's Priorities

Chapter 3

Written in February 2004

Selected Excerpts from *Where America Went Wrong*

Following are selected excerpts from "Where America Went Wrong", a book Talbott wrote and published in February 2004. The publisher was Financial Times Prentice Hall.

Truly we have a great gross national product...but can that be the criterion by which we judge this country? Is it enough? For the gross national product counts air pollution and cigarette advertising and ambulances to clear our highways of carnage. It counts special locks for our doors and jails for the people who break them. It counts Whitman's rifle and Speck's knife and television programs, which glorify violence in order to sell toys to our children. And the gross national product, the gross national product does not allow for the health of our children, the quality of their education, the joy of their play. It is indifferent to the decency of our factories and the safety of our streets alike. It does not include the beauty of our poetry or the strength of our marriages, the intelligence of our public debate or the integrity of our public officials. It measures neither wit nor courage, neither our wisdom nor our learning, neither our compassion nor our duty to our country. It measures everything, in short, except that which makes life worthwhile, and it can tell us everything about America, except why we are proud to be Americans.

Robert F. Kennedy
January 4, 1968

<u>Is It The Economy, Stupid?</u>

To begin a discussion of why democracy and free markets seem to be in apparent conflict today, an examination of what a supporter of completely free market capitalism might argue are the benefits of such an economic system is called for. For these purposes, this advocate will be identified as "the libertarian" because the point is to convey how a free market might operate properly with as little government interference as possible.

First, the libertarian would argue that history itself has demonstrated free market capitalism's superiority to any other economic system. Capitalism has created the greatest degree of wealth for those countries that have adopted it. Many empirical academic studies have indeed shown that per capita incomes are highest in countries with strong property rights and a rule of law, two essential elements of a capitalist system (Aron). Daron Acemoglu of the Massachusetts Institute of Technology (MIT) has retraced 500-year-old data to show that those countries that had the best institutions to protect private property centuries ago were those that have experienced the greatest growth since then. He makes a fairly good argument that the causality arrow goes from good institutions to greater economic growth and not the reverse.

If the polar opposite of capitalism is communism, the libertarian's case is strengthened because it is impossible to think of a single historic or current communist regime that did not degenerate into dictatorship and fairly low levels of economic output. The people of the former Soviet Union and Mao's China suffered enormous economic hardship, brutal working conditions and terrible loss of life during severe famines.

Even if one concedes that, on average, capitalist countries are more wealthy, how is this wealth shared across all the population? If all the wealth in a capitalist country resided in a few families' hands, then one could not claim that the average citizen was any better off or that poverty had been relieved.

In fact, wealth is not shared equally in capitalist countries. In a free-market system, there is no mechanism for ensuring that wealth is distributed equally, and the libertarian is glad there is not. The free-market libertarian depends on the freedom of the market to allow for various levels of individual effort, output and income rewards. He recognizes that no free-market system will reward everyone equally. He knows that life is not necessarily fair and that some have "unfair" economic or social advantages, schooling advantages, intellectual advantages or just incredible good luck that allows different people to achieve different levels of income under capitalism. The libertarian does not apologize for these differences; he applauds them. Such variances in income create, in the libertarian's argument, the motivations for underachievers to work harder and for the rich to invest the savings that will fund the next level of technological investment leading to even greater levels of productivity.

Somewhat surprisingly, based on an academic study that this author performed with Richard Roll of UCLA's Anderson School, countries of the world with stronger property rights, better enforced rules of law and higher per capita incomes, namely the more capitalist societies, seemed to have more egalitarian distributions of income across their citizenry (Roll and Talbott, 2002).

This finding flies in the face of conventional wisdom that says a higher-growth, more productive capitalist economic system invites large disparities of income. Roll and Talbott (2002) found no tradeoff was required between greater economic prosperity and more egalitarian distributions of income.

The libertarian would suggest another major benefit of a free-market system -- that it is self-policing. This means that inefficient and unproductive firms, companies and workers would be automatically weeded out by the system. The competitive free-market pricing system selects for the low-cost producer and has little to no sympathy for the high-cost producer. Regardless of how big a company is, how long it has been in business or who the chairman is, through its pricing mechanism the competitive marketplace rewards businesses that are efficient and productive. Firms that are deemed to be inefficient become unprofitable and eventually disappear.

While bankruptcies can be painful to the employees of the defunct firm, in the long term, from society's perspective, it is better if they find new jobs in which their skills and talents can create products and services that are truly valued by other citizens. The free market's greatest contribution to increased productivity may be this creative destruction process that allows financial and human resources to move fluidly to productive ventures.

The final argument by the libertarian on the benefits of capitalism might be the most disputed, namely, that capitalism turns greed from a vice into a virtue. Adam Smith in 1776 was the first to describe the "invisible hand" of capitalism in which all market participants, acting only in their narrow self-interest, maximize the good for everyone.

To summarize, the libertarian has argued that free-market capitalism has created the greatest degree of wealth for its country's citizens, the highest level of personal incomes, the fairest distribution of those incomes that still preserves the productive nature of the economy and the greatest alleviation of poverty in the world. Although many of these benefits result directly from industrialization, the libertarian argues that industrialization is most likely to occur in a free market society in which risk taking is rewarded and property rights are respected. The argument concludes by declaring capitalism has turned people's assumed natural greed from a vice to a virtue and that the self-policing nature of free markets preserves efficiency in the system.

This is probably an opportune time to introduce a hypothetical opponent to the stated positions of the libertarian who is referred to here simply as "the antiglobalist." It will be the antiglobalist's objective to find fault with the libertarian view that completely free economic markets are the ideal system to maximize human welfare and well-being. While it is impossible to stereotype an effort as diverse as the antiglobalization movement, this hypothetical spokesperson can at least argue the shortcomings of completely free-market capitalism.

First, the antiglobalist agrees it is difficult to find alternative economic systems that have created as much wealth as capitalism. She also agrees that communism seems to be a bankrupt concept. Still, the antiglobalist has not given up hope that there is another, as-yet-undiscovered economic system that will create the economic opportunities to allow every person to escape poverty and also do a better job of maintaining the human dignity and self-respect of every citizen. Finally, the antiglobalist hopes an economic system exists that doesn't measure all value and successes in dollars but recognizes many other human ambitions and emotions not easily captured in measuring the GDP.

Although not insisting on perfect equality of outcomes, the antiglobalist sees the wealthy of the world sitting on enormous assets and savings while the poorest starve. Free-market capitalism has no conscience, but people do. She believes that properly elected governments can interfere constructively with the free market on behalf of their people such that opportunities and outcomes will be more ethical, more just, and more fair than if the free market were allowed to dictate outcomes itself. She knows that this constructive interference must not be so blatant as to "kill the goose that laid the golden egg." In other words, government regulation cannot be so burdensome that it destructively interferes with the operation of the free market, and it cannot be so taxing that citizens, including the wealthiest, lose their motivation to work hard and productively.

Obviously, for governments to play this regulatory role, they must be powerful enough to enforce any regulation or taxation scheme the people feel is appropriate. The government must also have the ability to apply sanctions to the offenders. Therefore, the question is not whether to make government powerful; that is a requirement. The real question is how to limit the use of government power to prevent the government from itself coercing its own citizenry.

The idea that democratic governments elected by the people have the moral authority to step in and interfere with the operation of the free market is lost on most libertarians, especially when wealth or income redistribution schemes are discussed.

What is interesting is that libertarians do not like to admit that the free market could not function without government regulation and interference. Who enforces private contracts? The government. Who tries and sentences fraudulent company executives? The government. Who maintains the system of title and property records that the entire private property system is based on? The government. Businesses are very interested in having governments enforce patent, copyright and intellectual property laws. Why should antiglobalists not expect labor, environmental and consumer laws to be equally well enforced around the world?

So the decision is not *whether* the government will interfere in a free market but rather how much interference is appropriate. Again, somewhat surprisingly, Roll and Talbott (2003) found in their research that the richer more advanced countries of the world had bigger, not smaller, governments than their poorer neighbors, when government spending was measured as a percentage of gross domestic product (GDP). So, in contrast to typical IMF advice, one of the problems of developing countries is not that their governments are too big and need cutting back, but rather that many are too small and need reinforcing. As in Iraq recently, it is fruitless to talk about private enterprise development until there is a government in place sufficiently powerful to maintain law and order and create the proper governmental institutions required for economic development.

Neither the antiglobalist nor the libertarian wants government to get too big. They both know that government, unlike the free market, has very few self-policing mechanisms and that programs run by the government often end up being terribly inefficient because of a lack of competition. But the recent problems on Wall Street suggest that less regulation is not always the answer. As revealed with the problems at Enron, Global Crossing and Tyco, among others, U.S.

Securities and Exchange Commission (SEC) regulation is good because it attempts to ensure transparency of financial statements and prevent accounting fraud.

So the alternative economic model that the antiglobalist would like to propose is a free-market economy regulated by and reporting to a democratically-elected government. This is not a new concept; it is approximately where the United States was after the New Deal was enacted in the 1930s. What has happened since then, especially through globalization's opportunities for multinational firms to escape any one country's regulations is a return to a much freer, less regulated market system. Many of the advances of the New Deal have been rolled back, including unions' collective bargaining power, the ability of the government to effectively tax its corporations, the safety of Americans' pension and Social Security plans, the required separation of banks' debt and equity investments and so on. Often, regardless of whether big business, big government or labor was to blame for the various economic calamities that have occurred around the world, working men and women have been asked to shoulder the major burden of the recovery process through lower wages and fewer jobs. Any economic problem, from a weak economy to bad investment policies to too much corporate debt can easily be corrected by just lowering wages and waiting for profits to recover, if working people allow it.

Internationally speaking, many antiglobalists believe the major reason U.S. corporations move plants offshore has nothing to do with the theory of comparative advantage, but rather they are trying to avoid taxes, find cheap non-union labor, avoid environmental laws and duck government regulations regarding workplace safety and worker welfare (Greider). Globalization offers multinational corporations the opportunity to compete in an unregulated world where the only rules are written by nondemocratic organizations they control, such as the WTO. But as globalization proceeds, corporations have been allowed to ignore that economic participants must abide by rules established by a democratic government elected by the people. Corporations want no regulation, but the people of the world don't want multinational corporations running roughshod over them and their families. The basic democratic disconnect between free traders and antiglobalists is that once trade is encouraged between countries, it is not clear to which courts they answer, which multinational governmental body has authority to regulate, what democratic process gave that body its authority and which citizens of the world it reports to.

The antiglobalist has one more serious issue with free-market capitalism -- there are entire classes of goods and services that it does a very poor job of allocating (collective action issues and social good like justice). If the government were not involved and the free markets were left to work by themselves, these very important goods and services would be allocated terribly. Because the free-market system does a poor job allocating them fairly, the government should be involved in allocating them. And because government will determine their ultimate allocation, free-market participants bidding with dollars should not have undue influence in the government. This will become a primary reason to restrict corporations' and wealthy individuals' purchasing activities to the economic marketplace and to not allow them to bid for these other services in the political arena through the use of campaign donations and lobbying dollars.

So the antiglobalist has made some compelling arguments as to why free markets may not be the ideal allocation mechanism for all goods and services. Although capitalism is an economic model and democracy is a model of government, the two systems are much more intertwined than typically suggested. The antiglobalist has also argued that for moral reasons, when the two are in conflict, the government must have authority as the market is nothing more than a mechanism for allocating goods, and its greatest strength, its lack of moral objectivity, is also its greatest weakness. Only the people, operating through a well-functioning democracy, can lend an economic system the moral authority a society inevitably needs to function smoothly. America has trended recently to an ever-increasing free-market approach, especially with its emphasis on unregulated globalization, and because of this it has violated some of the basic precepts of how an economy must be regulated and organized to operate properly and maximize the welfare of its citizens.

It turns out that both free market capitalism and democratic forms of government are susceptible to corruptive influences in the real world (Mauro). Concentrated power tends toward corruption (Olson). In economics, it takes the form of monopoly power, and in a representative democracy, it assumes the role of a special interest. In each case, the powerful are trying to usurp a greater voice in the economy or the government than they deserve. A monopoly has more coercive power than its individual dollars might have in the marketplace, and the special interest has more influence over the government than is achievable through simple majority voting.

Because government best allocates non-economic goods and because everyone should actively participate in deciding how they are allocated, it makes no sense to allow anything but equal representation of all peoples when selecting one's elected representatives. Any system that allows unequal representation or undue influence of moneyed or special interests is therefore inherently unfair.

Is Government the Problem?

One current democracy in the world has a particularly offensive anti-democratic record:

History of subjugating women and minorities

Government founded by radicals and revolutionaries using guerrilla-like tactics

Individual freedoms and voting rights originally restricted to land-owning, older white males constituting less than 3% of overall population

Ninety-five percent of forestlands burned or destroyed by its citizenry, causing enormous environmental damage

Weapons of mass destruction utilized during war

Opposition to international treaties to limit global warming or try international war criminals

Impediment to international free trade with huge domestic agricultural and industrial subsidies

Economy is in disarray because of corporate corruption and accounting scandals

"Free" press owned and controlled by large multinational corporations

Use of preemptive "first-strike" attacks against foreign countries

Current leader seized office with assistance of highest court after losing popular vote (written in 2004).

Of course, this extremely "undemocratic" country is the United States of America. Many people criticize America, and to America's credit, many of the most critical are Americans. America is more open and freer than most countries, but recently there has been a greater disconnect between our government's actions and the wishes of its people. Surely, this has not been lost on our international allies who watch us in a state of puzzled bewilderment.

Representative democracy has grown to be an enormously popular form of government worldwide (Diamond). In this third century of America, however, many Americans have forgotten what it is about democracy that is so powerful. Certainly, one can recite platitudes about the individual liberty and freedom that democracy offers citizens, but our country's founders seemed to have a much better grasp of democracy's strengths and potential weaknesses than many Americans do today.

Primarily, democracy is a glorious tribute to the individual (Milton Friedman). In an 18th century world dominated by monarchs and God, founders drew on the writings of great Greek, French and English philosophers to create a government that celebrated the sanctity and authority of the people. People hold the right to control their own destiny; they cannot be ruled by governments unless they decide to grant certain powers to said governments to better conduct their affairs and preserve peace with their neighbors. All power comes from the people. No government can claim any moral authority unless it was duly elected by the public (William J. Talbott). Although democratic majorities in history have committed immoral acts, to date, no one has devised a better way of policing concentrations of political and economic power than by making them obedient to a democratic government freely elected by the majority of the people. Actions taken by the majority are not by definition moral, but actions taken by a leader must have majority backing before they can be considered to represent the will of the people and be judged as moral. There is no such moral test or moral authority attached to autocrats acting alone; history has taught us they often act in their own self-interest regardless of what their stated intentions are. Unfortunately, democracies have not figured out how to also guarantee the right of minorities within a democratic society (John Stuart Mill).

Our founders quickly realized the dilemma they faced in creating a government powerful enough to protect and punish, yet not so powerful that it came to prey on its own citizens. Their solution was to give the federal government very broad powers to protect citizens from coercion, but also to try to restrain it so as to protect individual freedoms. Any secondary school student can tell you they achieved this through a division of state and federal powers, a separation of federal power into three branches and a constitution and bill of rights that expressly stated and guaranteed the rights of the individual. Many

Americans believe today that government has grown too big and that big government itself is the problem facing America.

Libertarians in the U.S. who wish to limit government power further might argue that our founders failed to put real constraints on the elected terms of our representatives, the size of government, its borrowing capacity or its ability to run large operating deficits. But thanks to the wisdom of our founders, a procedure is in place for these good citizens to correct those oversights. Our constitution is amendable. The uncontrolled and unresponsive nature of government today is just another symptom of a more fundamental problem facing our country; our democracy is broken.

Rather than require every citizen to spend every day studying every issue needing government attention, the country's founders decided to allow representatives or agents to do the bidding of the people for them. Of course, they recognized they were granting enormous decision making power to these representatives, and recalling that absolute power corrupts, they tried to make these representatives responsive to the people by making them stand for election at regular intervals. That was 215 years ago, and then we went to sleep.

What has happened since to our wonderful ideal of democracy? Forces outside of government have tried to corruptly grab power for themselves. In addition, those good-hearted representatives we elected have acted in their own self-interest to free themselves of the bonds of accountability and have tried to consolidate their power for their own selfish goals. This is the classic principal/agent problem in which agents begin to act in their own self-interest rather than their clients', as clients do not want to spend the time and energy to conduct the business themselves. Under such a system, it is natural to assume that principals will allow a certain amount of corrupt activity by agents before deeming it worth their time to get involved and clean things up. In America, now is that time!

Elected representatives in America have concocted a wonderful system over the years to ensure their reelection regardless of how unresponsive they are to their constituents. The most egregious component of this is accepting large campaign donations in exchange for political favors. These are nothing more than bribes and they occur every day in Washington and in our state capitals. If not bribes, why would defense companies give monies to congressmen who sit on the defense appropriation committees? But many of our elected representatives don't stop there. They make it a near certainty that they will be re-elected and that their power remains absolute. They have fought against public funding of campaigns as it might eliminate some of the inherent advantages of incumbency. And in what must be one of the most unethical acts a democracy has seen, representatives have re-carved their congressional districts through gerrymandering schemes to ensure that their biggest supporters remain in their district and potential opposition forces are discarded to someone else's.

It is ironic that corporations and the wealthy elite choose to interfere in the operation of a representative democracy. It turns out they might have the most to lose, economically speaking, if democracies are prevented from operating efficiently and properly. New empirical research by Roll and Talbott shows that well-functioning democratic institutions such as voting rights, civil liberties and freedom of speech are each highly correlated across the countries of the world with higher average country incomes. The research yielded strong evidence that democratic reforms cause economic growth and not that greater prosperity creates its own demand for better democracy. If correct, the study suggests that greater democracy is not a hindrance to greater economic growth but, indeed, might be a fundamental force in the promotion and sustainability of a prosperous economy. Rather than fight the pro-democracy protestors in the street with tear gas, corporations and wealthy elites should invite them into their WTO, IMF and World Bank meetings. They should offer them tea and cookies and welcome them to a new alliance to expand world economies and conquer world poverty through properly regulated "free trade" and democracy.

Recently, the wealthy's steamrolling of the passage of tax cuts for the rich through congress appeared to benefit them in the short run, but if society or the economy is permanently damaged the wealthy could be the biggest losers. How short-sighted of the wealthy elite if, in grabbing $3.8 trillion of tax cuts in the short run they create a government deficit so big that it retards economic growth and thus reduces the value of their own stock portfolios in the future. The economy received a temporary Keynesian bounce due to the increased spending associated with the tax cuts, but as of this writing, there was no pick-up in either long-term economic growth prospects or new job creation.

Economics grow organically, from the bottom up. This means that a healthy economy needs individuals and small business owners excited about investing in new product opportunities, expanding their businesses, maintaining their homes and investing in their children's education (DeSoto). Education enhances the total value of human capital just as building a new factory increases physical capital (Barro).

How powerful is democracy in stimulating bottom-up growth? When it is allowed to operate, it can be very effective. Raghuram G. Rajan and Luigi Zingales in their new book, *Saving Capitalism from the Capitalists* (2003), make the point that some advanced economies may have suffered from granting too much power to the biggest incumbent companies and industries to the detriment of entrepreneurship and innovation. In such an economy, big traditional businesses are prevented from failing by means of their hammer lock on government and industry allies (Shleifer). Properly functioning democracy will break that stranglehold of business on government by allowing the general populace to make the rules. Such top-down control of the government and the economy by powerful industry incumbents would be forbidden in a true bottom-up democracy.

What type of instability do capitalists fear when they talk about democracy? They have a fear that greater democracy will lead to greater power for the masses and with it a greater demand for "un-economic" property, land, wealth and income redistributions. First, these economists have missed the whole point that some income and wealth redistribution may be completely moral and a positive development for the well-being of the economy depending on how skewed income and wealth distributions have become. In trying to defend the sanctity of the free market system, namely, strong property rights and laws, they have failed to realize that a fairer sharing of economic and political power may lead to a more stable, more inclusive, more productive society. If a large percentage of a population feels disenfranchised, how can these citizens begin to feel excited about investing in that economy.

There is a second danger some capitalists perceive in full participatory democracy. Many people just don't trust or respect the judgments of other citizens. Even our founders thought non-land owners might lack sufficient intellect and motivation to understand and respect a government of the people and an economy that protected property rights. Today, many of us, even if we don't like to admit it, are intellectual, cultural, racial or ethnic elites. We don't mind giving the vote to our own kind, but we are suspicious of those unlike ourselves.

Clearly, holding politicians accountable for their promises, keeping them targeted on the electorate's welfare and needs and protecting government against inefficiency and wastefulness are all extremely important. But the most important function of a democracy may be to limit corruption in government and the private sector. How else but with the constant self-policing of a democracy can any system of accumulated power be constrained to act in the public's interest rather than its own? Corruption is enormously hurtful to the proper functioning of an economy (Mauro). Contracts much be honored, property must be protected from thieves, courts must provide just and fair decisions and legislators must act to improve the general welfare of the people (Clague).

Milton Friedman said that a major benefit of democracy is that it limits the power of centralized governments. Just as a free market economic system removes much of the pricing, purchasing and economic decision making from government, a voting democracy removes much of the political decision making from government bureaucrats. To the extent that centralized government is more likely to be remote from the electorate, it is much more likely to have confused its own self-interests with the public interest.

Corporations are Not Citizens!

If the greatest harm to our democracy is the undue influence of special interests, then the biggest and most powerful and most destructive special interest is corporate America. Undue influence of corporations on the government prevents the government from operating properly, but it also results in unfair advantages to these same corporations in the private marketplace. Who would have thought that the one thing that is wrong with the government -- undue influence on our democracy --would create the major problem facing the economy -- namely, unfair economic advantage granted to the largest corporate contributors and lobbyists? If we can return democracy to the government, the economy should also improve resulting in the best of both worlds.

How is it that, theoretically, capitalism can be our friend and yet actual corporations are not our friends? Corporations provide a tremendous function in the business world as an organizing structure that allows seamless cooperative effort among many individuals of the same firm. Corporations also ease transactions with third parties that can rely on corporate reputations to honor contracts and perform work as promised. Further, corporations allow joint ownership by shareholders who can then effortlessly, and without interference in business operations, monetize their ownership positions by selling their shares in a free market. This system assigns market values to firms based on the capitalization of future expected earnings and creates enormous liquidity that allows resources to flow to those with the best available projects.

The problem with corporations becomes apparent when they enter the political arena. Some might argue that corporations are just like other market participants and should be able to be represented in the government just like individuals who happen to own their own businesses. There is even an argument that perhaps corporations should have a more than equal share of representation because they know best how to manage things, they control most of the productive resources in a society and they hire the majority of its citizens.

Corporations should not have a disproportionate representation in the government. In fact, corporations should have no say in the government. They should not be allowed to contribute to the candidates, run political ads or lobby the government. The simple reason is that corporations are not people or citizens, but to see the point clearly, one must examine their function and structure. Only then will people gain an appreciation for why corporations should be restricted from the political arena and limited in their actions solely to the economic marketplace.

Why are corporations naturally at odds with the average workers in the country? It so happens that the biggest expense item for almost all corporations, and the line item that depresses corporate profits the most is wages. Corporations are in business to make profits, so it becomes one of their overriding objectives to reduce wages and eliminate unnecessary workers. Although this goal may be good for overall efficiency, you can see how it might not be the best thing for workers in the short run.

In addition to working for corporations, American citizens are all consumers of their products. Again, corporations are interested in producing products at the least possible cost while consumers may be more concerned with product safety, product quality and performance characteristics. Our interests are not aligned all the time, so it makes little sense to give the corporation an undue say in how government regulates products and ensures product safety.

Finally, some argue that what is good for General Motors (GM) is good for Americans. At one time, this might have been true. Henry Ford understood that if he paid a decent and living wage, his workers would be able to afford to buy his automobiles. But in a world where GM builds its cars and hires its workers overseas and yet sells them here, the economic link between what is good for GM and what's good for the American worker is much weaker. Even the profits of GM do not necessarily stay in America because its stock is owned by investors the world over.

An astute reader might argue that the world would be more efficiently structured if run by corporations' owners than by workers. Owners care about profits while employees care about jobs. Corporations' economic influence need not be limited as long as it is constrained by appropriate antitrust laws and other appropriate regulations because corporations have indeed been great agents of economic wealth creation. But in the world of politics and government their accumulation of power has no place.

The primary reason that corporations' influence must be constrained to the economic business arena and prohibited from affecting our political and governmental institutions is that corporations are, by definition, economic animals. Their charters, their bylaws, the commercial code and judicial precedence have all established that the sole purpose and responsibility of a public corporation, its executives and its board of directors is to maximize its share price (Hillman and Keim). Maximizing shareholder value encompasses many valuable economic benefits -- such as maximizing profits, cash flow and growth prospects as well as minimizing risk, but these are solely economic terms that may or may not improve the well-being of the overall citizenry. In a speech at Loyola University of Chicago, Roberto Goizueta, the former CEO of Coca Cola, argued that business has a role in creating a "civil society" in which social ills are successfully addressed.

It is fine that corporations as business entities seek to maximize profits and growth, but there is no corollary that says these goals alone will make society better off or that they should become society's overreaching goals and objectives. Economic prosperity is an important component of society's ability to provide for its citizens' well-being, but it is just one way to measure that well-being. Clearly there are others. Peace is an obvious goal of most individuals in a society, but it runs counter to the profit-maximizing goals of a defense contractor. It's not that defense contractors would start a war to sell more arms, but their self-interest may push them to favor violent resolutions to conflicts that might otherwise be resolved peacefully.

The joy that an individual experiences from family life can never be measured in terms of corporate profits. The love of family and children is clearly a benefit not captured in any stock price. And yet corporations can ask their employees to work longer hours sacrificing time with their families. Should these corporations have a disproportionate voice in our government in deciding required overtime or marital leave policies?

People take great joy in the arts and culture. Must museums be profitable to demonstrate their value to society? Is the worth of a Picasso captured solely in its resale value?

In addition to corporations' narrow economic focus, a primary difference between humans and corporations is that humans have the capacity for compassion and sympathy. When was the last time you heard a corporation called sympathetic? Even if the individual executives are sympathetic, their own charter would prevent their acting in any way but in the corporation's self-interest to maximize its own shareholder value.

Compassion and sympathy are extremely important in government affairs because a great deal of government's work is deciding how to treat the less fortunate; the elderly, the sick, the dying, the orphaned and the poor. Remember that the people in a properly functioning democracy should make only those decisions that are handled poorly by the free market. How could a corporation make these decisions? When a government is deciding issues of fairness and justice, what possible input could an amoral corporation have? In structuring rules of law and rights of property, why would a corporation suggest anything fair and reasonable to the entire society when it could easily jimmy the rules to increase its own profits?

No, a major role of government is to decide issues of fairness and justice, to establish fair rules and to compassionately care of its less fortunate citizens. Corporations are poorly equipped to deal with any of these issues, and if asked to or given the opportunity to lobby the government, they will do what they were set up to do, which is to try to bend the rules to increase their economic advantage. Corporations are amoral and competitive by their very nature. This is exactly why they are so successful economically and why it is inappropriate to ask them to participate in government affairs.

We need not guess what favors corporations would ask for if given the opportunity to contribute monies to politicians and lobby them for favors. The written record exists. The U.S. has had an open policy of allowing hard and soft money contributions from corporations for years and corporate lobbyists have always been welcome in Washington. The current challenges to existing campaign finance laws are based on the theory that a corporation wouldn't give money to a politician if it didn't expect something in return. As you might expect, first on their wish list is tax relief. One of the best investments a corporate CEO can make is the funding of a campaign contribution in exchange for tax relief. On average, the typical investment dollar spent on funding a politician's campaign or political party is returned over 360-fold in reduced taxes. A typical company today makes an average donation of $3.6 million and receives tax breaks equal to about $1.3 billion. If you could make investments with that kind of return you would make Warren Buffet look like a "piker." Three hundred sixty times your investment, every year, is a 36,000% annual return, which is not bad when Treasury securities are yielding 3.7%.

In addition to specific tax deductions like accelerated depreciation, corporations receive enormous tax subsidies -- literally direct payments from the federal government. According to Palast, they can also receive these other benefits in addition to tax advantages:

Price support help
Tariff protection
A granting or preservation of monopoly status
Import protection
Liberal export policies
Favorable regulations passed
Relief from onerous environmental laws
Restrictions on mandatory employee benefits
Pension funding relief
Liability protection
A supportive government when it comes time to fight workers' rights to unionize

To put the value of these "softer" benefits in perspective, let's examine just the last one, the ease with which workers might be able to unionize. The percentage of private sector wage and salary workers who are unionized in this country has dropped dramatically during the last 50 years from over 35% to approximately10% (U.S. Bureau of Labor Statistics). There are many reasons for this decline, but a contributing factor may be the laws regulating union organizing and the regulatory difficulties involved in setting up a union shop. The laws were changed in favor of management in the 1950s, and union participation percentages have been declining ever since. It is not a coincidence that union organizing became a much more legally challenging task during a period in which corporate America dramatically stepped up its lobbying and election donation efforts in Washington.

It is in corporations' interests to limit the power of unions. Imagine, hypothetically, that an anti-union corporate lobbying effort in Washington resulted in a decline of $1 per hour in real wages for all workers in the country. It seems reasonable to assume that non-union workers might suffer any wage decline suffered by union workers as their pay often tracks that of union workers in any particular industry. It turns out the real wages have indeed stagnated during the last 25 years, with little to no real increase at all during the period (U.S. Bureau of Labor Statistics).

If corporations were able to accomplish this assumed $1 decrease in wages (or if they have accomplished it already), it represents an enormous transfer of wealth from workers to shareholders of large corporations. There are approximately 140 million workers in this country (U.S. Census Bureau) working 36 hours a week on average (U.S. Bureau of Labor Statistics). This means a $1 per hour cut in all wages represents over $250 billion per year savings to all corporations (assuming for this rough estimation that everybody works for a corporation).

If these annual pretax cost savings (which are almost the same as after-tax savings because many corporations in the U.S. pay no federal income tax) were capitalized at an assumed average stock market multiple of 15 times, their theoretical market capitalizations might increase by as much as $3.7 trillion. This $3.7 trillion represents no new wealth -- just a shift from employees' pockets to shareholders' stock values. It would, however, cause an increase of approximately 25% in the value of the entire stock market. What many people do not realize is that the stock market captures the values due shareholders but ignores whether these values are newly created from an exciting new product or merely a transfer of wealth from another constituency such as the employees to the shareholders. Clearly, it pays to lobby your representatives in Washington. Do you think this might explain a major portion of the bull market during the Reagan era, which was decidedly anti-union right from the start? Remember, stock markets increasing in value say nothing about the condition or welfare of the respective workers or citizens.

When people make judgments about whether corporations and wealthy individuals are fairly earning their profits, they must remember that profits are highly dependent on the rules of the game. Many libertarians believe there is something natural or God given about free markets and the rules currently governing them. This is not true. Not that the rules are arbitrary, but they are very much subject to influence and revision. To see the point, ask a libertarian why there are patent laws and then ask whether patents should be protected for 17 years, 40 years or forever. Rather than being arbitrary, the proper patent life should maximize innovation by protecting inventors, but not act as a constraint in the long term on the distribution of new technologies beneficial to mankind. Having seen multinational pharmaceutical companies' reluctance to make AIDS drugs available to the developing world should convince the reader that corporations are not the best judges of societal and civic responsibility.

Give me one hour in Washington and I could change the rules by which the economic game is played such that corporate profitability either went to zero or doubled, depending solely on how I fixed the laws of commerce. It is extremely important that all citizens have great confidence that the rules are being set fairly and justly and, yes, morally as well. Without this confidence, average citizens will not have the incentive to put their own capital at risk and invest in the game. If the rules were not fair, who would ever want to play the game and invest time and money? But without new investment dollars, the game is over. That is why it is critical that corporations not be allowed to influence how these rules are written. If Americans continue to allow corporate influence in Washington, they have themselves to blame when corporations use that power to grab more than their fair share of the economic pie. And Americans will have created the means by which the government sacrifices all quality of life and fairness issues in a constant effort to keep the corporate "fat cats" happy.

All currently successfully operating businesses share one attribute; they are incumbents and, as such, they all fear future competitors that might eventually strain their profit margins or bankrupt them. Therefore, it is in the interest of all well-established businesses to lobby our government to reinforce the status quo. One would expect them to be against innovation, against small business formation and most definitely against allowing companies like themselves to fail through bankruptcy. They would naturally be in favor of whatever government support they could garner to avoid having to claim bankruptcy. But the continued existence of money-losing firms not only drains public funds that go to their life support, it also ties up valuable people and physical resources that might be better utilized in a different industry or business. When firms go bankrupt, capital and human resources move out of slow to no growth companies and industries and weak managements and inefficient operations are eliminated.

There is no hard academic evidence to date that shows bankruptcies are bad for an economy (Richard Roll). But companies approaching bankruptcy ask Congress to save them, saying they are concerned not with themselves, but only with their employees, even if the management team in question hasn't thought of its employees once in the last decade without thinking about how it might take them for another nickel of pay. Society would be much better off if it allowed these poorly-run firms to fail. Many of their employees will do fine finding new jobs, and if it is unconstrained by corporate lobbying, the government can be more generous with unemployment insurance plans so that the displaced who are unsuccessful in job placement immediately do not suffer harshly.

Allowing bankruptcies also serves notice to the rest of corporate America that the game is being played fairly and by the rules. If you do stupid things and take stupid risks in your business, you will not have the American taxpayer around to bail you out. This is an incredibly important concept to an economy because businesses must understand there are repercussions to taking bigger and bigger risks. Without the implied threat of bankruptcy, managements would naturally be steered toward riskier projects that probably would not match the risk profile of the companies' shareholders.

With corporations allowed to attack the societal and political fabric of America with their greedy campaign donations and lobbying, all Americans will be worse off. There will be some or all of the following:

Less entrepreneurial activity
Less new business formation
Less new job growth
Less government oversight
More corruption
Less transparency
More emphasis on the status quo and less on innovation
A great deal of resources wasted on old industries and old ideas
Less voice for workers and citizens

This lobbying represents not only an unfair attempt to redistribute the country's precious resources but also a direct attack on America's democracy and our economy. It is an attack on our system of fairness and justice, the things an economy needs to encourage investment, the lifeblood of profitability and growth. If people lose confidence in their government's ability to make the rules of the game fair and applicable to all, they will vote with their feet (La Porta et al.).

Personal savings will decline and personal investment will decline. People will spend less time on their own educational investment. Over time, the rich would get richer and the poor would have trouble keeping up. This is exactly what has been happening in America for the last 25years.

Corporations lobbied for open U.S. borders and legal and illegal immigration into the U.S., especially of unskilled workers, mushroomed. The same corporations lobbied for global trade and now American workers are in competition with poorly organized workers the world over. As a result, U.S. workers' wages stagnated while executives' compensation packages soared. Unions became less important, union membership declined, and union wages, benefits and work rules suffered. It became more difficult for minimum wage laws to keep up with inflation.

There is not a great deal of time to act to address the problem of excessive corporate lobbying and corporations' unjust campaign contributions., Very soon it will get to the point where any dissent along these lines either goes unheard or will be reported as un-American. The future, unfortunately, may already be here. Nothing is as un-American as what big corporations are doing to the American people and their freedom by the undue and unwanted influence of big business on our democratic government.

Our Country's Problems and the Special Interest Groups Chosen to Solve Them

Problem And Current Problem Solver

Failure of schools - Teachers union
Election laws - Incumbents
Corporate corruption - Accounting firms
Military spending - Defense contractors
Global warming   - Coal-fired utilities
Drug costs - Pharmaceutical companies
Social security - AARP
Complex tax code - IRS
Zoning laws - Real estate developers
Tobacco restrictions - Tobacco companies
Palestinian conflict - Jewish lobby
Gas mileage - Auto manufacturers

Justice system - Lawyers
Wages and benefits - Unions
Legalized gambling - Casinos
Government excess - Government workers

While competition is good for the economic marketplace, cooperation is the key to good government policies. And to cooperate effectively, everyone needs to share the pain to some degree. This will be much easier to do after fairness is instilled back into the system through elimination of undue influence in the government. In such a world, the true greatness of Americans and their generous and cooperative spirit will once again dominate petty politics.

If you agree that the story told so far in this text is an extremely important and disturbing one, you might ask why it wasn't exposed sooner. The American government depends on a two-party system in which each party should be anxious to expose bad behavior on the part of the other. Unfortunately, both parties are feeding from the same trough. Their candidates depend on corporate and special interest monies to help them get reelected. One can't expect an incumbent to rat on another incumbent because they both are benefiting enormously from the system.

There is a far wider story of influence and power, far beyond the halls of Congress. It would not be sufficient for the most powerful in our country to be able to try to influence the government unfairly if the country's media or academia could easily blow the whistle on this abuse of democracy.

But how could corporations and the wealthy have acted to prevent the media or academia from playing their roles as watchdog to our democracy? One might assume there was some sort of secret conspiracy in which corporations quietly overtook our colleges and our news media. Here, however, activities were much more out in the open. You don't have to believe in secret initiation rituals at the Skull and Bones Society at Yale, strange Masonic meetings held in the dead of night, a Trilateral Commission, or even a New World Order to understand how big corporations and the wealthy were able to organize their efforts effectively to corrupt our government and influence our media and our academics.

Has Academia Lost Its Independence?

Universities, first and foremost, should be centers of learning and the acquisition of knowledge. History has taught us that both teaching and learning proceed best when the environment is free of bias and prejudice. Every university should be a free marketplace of ideas. Free speech rights are of the utmost importance everywhere in a democracy, but probably nowhere are they as important as on a university campus. University professors and students must feel free to express their ideas if true learning is to occur. It is in the very nature of the evolution of knowledge that arguments are required to hash out new ideas, that these new ideas must replace the old. Such regeneration is inhibited if there is a bias toward a particular approach or belief, especially the status quo.

Universities, in addition to providing a haven for the discussion of new and oftentimes unpopular ideas, have a very important role to play in a well-functioning democracy. Academics occupy an important place in society because they are regarded as intelligent, knowledgeable, expert and generally unbiased. (The fact that academics themselves realize this makes it sometimes difficult for them to embrace the democratic idea that everyone's vote should be treated equally. Sometimes, because of their own great personal investment in knowledge, they are slow to understand the reasoning of a democracy that says every person's vote should be equal. In a sense, this makes them intellectual elites and as such they have to be sure they don't inhibit democratic reforms in order to protect their privileged positions.)

This highly regarded status is conferred by society because citizens believe that academics work very hard for less than they might earn in the real world and historically have worked hard to preserve their intellectual independence. Their independent status, unbiased perspective and huge reservoir of intellect and knowledge lead professors often to be called as expert witnesses in court trials and are the reason their letters to the editors of America's newspapers carry such weight. Citizens and courts trust and respect their views because they presume those views to be independently generated, to speak for the public good and not to have any secret or undisclosed other interest or master to serve.

Because Americans believe them to be unbiased, they often turn to their universities when confronting dilemmas facing the republic and their beloved democracy. They assume an academic will arrive at a fair solution, having no axe to grind. And academics have often played important roles as fact-checkers and overseers of the operations of the government and the business community. The antiwar protest movement during the Vietnam conflict is but one example of a moral initiative that started on college campuses across the country. Much of the support for the civil rights movement, the women's movement and the attack on global sweatshops can be traced back to campuses. If universities were to lose their unbiased moral compass the loss would be felt by not only students but by the entire democracy. Unions, churches and the media also try to play this oversight role to some degree, but they all carry with them particular ingrained biases that make their roles more suspect.

It is probably fair to say that most universities historically have had a liberal bias. But in the last 30 years, this has begun to change. Although there are still many liberals on college campuses, there is a new breed of professor who is much more comfortable with, and closer to, business and industry. Many reside in the nation's business schools that at least practice full disclosure in identifying themselves as associated with a "business" school. Being pro-business is not necessarily a bad thing -- only when it gets in the way of a professor's ability to think freely and speak freely should alarms sound. A professor's particular belief system is his own business, but when industry interferes on campus to try to sway professors' opinions and views with dollars and prestigious opportunities and assignments then one should be concerned.

The most important task most university presidents have on campus today is not recruiting excellent students or professors but raising money for the university's endowment. Even many state-supported schools have moved to an endowment structure to assist in filling in the gaps left by government funding cutbacks. Therefore, successful university presidents today are more likely to be those with strong business and investment skills and good relationships with the business community.

Where does the money come from to fund an endowment? If it is not coming directly from a corporation or a corporate foundation, it is most likely coming from an alumnus who works or worked at a corporation. In today's world, corporations and their executives control most of the purse strings on campus. You can see the danger. It is very important to know what promises a university is making to attract this corporate largesse. If capital contributed to the school has contingencies attached to it, it can make the independent running of the school difficult if not impossible. Once the school accepts monies from a corporate donor and applies them toward the school's operating budget, that donor has incredible leverage over how that school acts in the future. There is no law against a corporate donor making demands in exchange for funding, but it can weaken the independence that every school desires and craves.

Lawrence Soley, in his book *Leasing the Ivory Tower: The Corporate Takeover of Academia*, gives a rather minor example of Glassboro State College, which accepted a $100 million gift from Henry M. Rowan in 1992. Part of the money was to be used for student scholarships for children of Rowan's company's employees, but only non-union employees. Given the magnitude of the total gift, Glassboro State College officials decided initially to accept this discriminatory condition, but union and media pressure eventually forced Rowan to reverse his original position and allow the funds to be used for all employees' children. Is it not amazing how fuzzy our logic becomes when someone dangles $100 million in front of us?

In a more prominent case in 2000, Phil Knight, the CEO of Nike, Inc. announced he was withdrawing his commitment to give $30 million to the University of Oregon, his alma mater. He was upset because, against his urging, the university had decided to join the Worker Rights Consortium (WRC). This organization looks into the unfair treatment of workers in sweatshops around the world, primarily in the footwear and apparel industries. Not by coincidence, these are the two largest business sectors for Knight's firm.

The University's action had the full support of students and faculty. It was an incredibly important issue to the students because surveys had shown that much of the apparel and footwear produced in these sweatshops was being sold on college campuses often at school-sponsored bookstores. Here was an ideal opportunity for students to feel some sense of solidarity and compassion with workers halfway around the world who seemed to need their assistance. Besides teaching important participatory democratic principles, what university would not be proud if it could teach its students the simple lesson of human compassion?

In time, Knight became a financial supporter of the school's football team again, but not before the Oregon's Board of Higher Education ruled that the university could not join an organization such as the WRC. Supposedly, the reason Knight reversed his decision never to support the school again was not a plea from the president or the dean of students, but a threat from the football coach to move to Ohio State unless Knight resumed his financial support.

In an even more disturbing trend, corporate contributions and monies are finding their way directly onto campuses. For a reasonable price, a corporate or wealthy private donor can fund a named academic chair, a department, a new wing, a building, a stadium or an entire school. It must be hard to have to try to conduct unbiased research with a corporate name, the name of a Wall Street titan or an industry's moniker on a professor's business card. Try acting and teaching without bias when your official title is: "The K-Mart Professor of Marketing and Business Strategy." Professors would only be acting rationally if they began to ease up on any work critical of either business in general or the industry or company funding their chairs. In a world where Americans are concerned when their city's stadium is renamed after a corporation, why is there no outrage when their institutions of higher learning are sold to the highest bidder? Americans shouldn't care much if Michael Jordan has been bought by Nike, but they should definitely care if Nike has purchased their academic elite.

Professors' relationships with corporate America are not limited to the partial funding of their salaries. Many professors make multiples of their base salaries from consulting relationships they have in the private sector. A general rule on most campuses is that professors can spend 20% of their work time on these consulting assignments, supposedly because spending time in the real world keeps the academic current. The problem is that professors so dependent on consulting gigs will be very slow to say or write anything critical of business. Active academic consultants become very friendly with their corporate hosts who often fund expensive trips to faraway conferences and even act as sources of funding for academic publication needs.

A specific type of consulting that academics provide is giving expert testimony at trials. Even if academics act completely ethically in arriving at their expert advice, they may be very unlikely to risk this income stream by doing or saying anything against corporate entities because big corporations make the best repeat clients. Some of these experts are paid tens of thousands of dollars per day for their testimony. There is great pressure to have the testimony come out the way one's employer wishes it to. It is not proper to assign blame to all members of academia, but one only has to observe professors giving expert testimony funded by the tobacco industry that tobacco products are not addictive to see there is a real problem.

In addition to consulting practices, many professors in medicine, biology, physics, business and computer science have established their own businesses, often in partnership with corporate America. The innovations and research that many academics are in the business of generating are easily turned into profit-making patentable businesses. In partnership with biotech, computer chip, pharmaceutical, brokerage and defense companies, these small jointly-owned companies have enormous upside potential. While it is wonderful to see academics benefiting from their inventions, this kind of activity reinforces the bonds between academia and business and further invites conflicts of interest and bias onto campus. As my professor friend told me, "Isn't the first job of a university professor to teach?" Professors can easily move into the private sector if their primary interest is research or business.

In addition to teaching, universities act as the primary facility for conducting long-term research in America. Although it is helpful to have relationships with industry to ensure that this research has some practicality, society pays a high price if these relationships are too close. First, industry is not interested in very long-term research for research's sake. Corporations want earnings, and preferably in the next quarter. And yet it is exactly this kind of long-term research that incubates entire new processes, products, companies and industries. Second, and not surprisingly, published research funded by a particular industry is rarely, if ever, critical of that industry. While most professors are ethically above actually changing the results of an experiment to support a sponsor, it is amazing how powerful self-deception is when the results are interpreted. People see what they want to see.

Just as disturbing is the practice of not publishing results that either refute or fail to support a sponsor's position. It is easy for many researchers to either redo the experiment or make subtle changes until they achieve more sponsor-friendly results. Most troublesome are contractual agreements with the sponsor that prevent releasing data without their approval -- a condition that ensures only pro-sponsor evidence will ever be released publicly. Finally, how could researchers not feel an ethical obligation to disclose the source of their funding if it is material to the research? Wouldn't people want to know that research conducted to measure the harmful effects of smoking was being funded by Phillip Morris?

Lawrence Solely reports that the amount of corporate research money going to universities increased fivefold during the 1980s. He cites a rather egregious example of corporate access and influence at MIT. There professors earn "bonus points" if they are supportive of the school's efforts to attract corporate involvement on campus. Professors get one point for providing an unpublished research paper to a corporation, two points for a corporate phone conversation and 12 points for a visit to a corporate headquarters. Each point can be redeemed for prizes and each is worth approximately $35.

Unfortunately, no points are given for showing up to class on time, updating last year's notes before giving a lecture, telling a great joke in class, scheduling office time to speak to students or writing a piece of research that truly revolutionizes the way people think about their place in the world. Thankfully, many such points-based incentive award programs have found to be rather ineffective in changing long-term human behavior.

The impact of corporate influence on campuses appears to be growing It has affected the curriculum of the schools, lessened the importance of teaching as research has become more highly emphasized, reduced academic freedom, strained professorial ethics, and damaged the sterling reputations of some of the country's finest institutions of higher learning. Derek Bok, the former president of Harvard, provides further testimony to the ever-increasing commercialization of our university campuses in his excellent text, *Universities in the Marketplace: The Commercialization of Higher Education.*

The influence of corporations on college campuses is not so pervasive that it has completely changed the culture of America's universities. But for it to do damage to America's democracy, it does not have to be ubiquitous. It need only establish a foothold such that one or two professors can conduct phony favorable research, give supportive, but false, expert testimony, and write enthusiastic op-ed pieces sympathetic to a company's cause without being shut down by the administration. If this is allowed to happen a few bad professors will have cashed in on and destroyed an academic reputation that took generations to build. One or two bad apples can most definitely spoil the bunch. The problem with impeccable reputations is they can easily be destroyed even if the vast majority of academia continues to honor their oaths by performing to the highest ethical standards. If a few damage the sanctity of academia, then all who did not act early to straighten out this problem will have to share in the blame.

Historically, citizens turned to university professors for an educated and unbiased opinion about the effects of new governmental laws and regulations and for their views on new political and economic agendas. The universities now have competition. The last 30 years has seen an explosion of think tanks, located both on and off college campuses. Most of these institutions are conservative, and the most popular causes they fight for are tax relief, free markets and a strong defense establishment.

To call think tanks research institutes is a misnomer. These institutions get almost all of their financial backing from wealthy conservative individuals and corporations. There was never a piece of "research" that these institutions completed that did not support their basic philosophy. This either is the luckiest streak of experiments in history, all providing supporting evidence that their organization's philosophy is universally correct -- which is very unlikely -- or offers proof that their research and reporting are extremely biased. Could you imagine working at a privately funded think tank and trying to publish an article directly contradicting the philosophy of your boss, your company, its founders and its financial backers? You would not only lose face, you would probably lose the job that goes along with that face. This demonstrates how important academic freedom is at our universities. If professors detect even a hint of an administration bias, their self-deception will work overtime to achieve an intellectual position that guarantees their job preservation.

The biggest off-campus conservative think tanks are the American Enterprise Institute (AEI), the Heritage Foundation, the Center for Strategic and International Studies (CSIS) and the Cato Institute, all conveniently headquartered in Washington. It is convenient because it is not research, but lobbying that these institutions are in the business of. The employees of these think tanks are often called "scholars" in an attempt to polish their reputations, but many are either unemployed lobbyists or ex-government employees. To make their work appear more scholarly, the think tanks have started their own "research" journals, although there is little to no peer review required to have an article published there. The AEI's journal, *Public Opinion* and the Heritage Foundation's, *Policy Review*, may sound just academic enough to fool the general public. University professors lend their institutions' reputations to these phony journals by agreeing to write articles for them, for a fee of course.

Conservative think tanks have discovered that dollars equals research. As long as you don't feel compelled to report all your results, you can continue to conduct experiments and basic research until you find support for your philosophy -- that is, as long as you are well funded. Not only do increased dollars create the potential for false research, but a well-funded marketing machine can see to it that your phony research will be in the hands of every congressional representative and on the nightly news while the theoretically correct research of the opposition languishes in the back of a less-well-financed, but real, academic research journal in the campus library.

So the wealthy and the corporations are creating their own scientific evidence and building their own "academic" institutions to buttress their worldview. There ought to be a law. Such fraudulent lobbying of Congress ought to carry the same penalties as false advertising for consumer products. People ought to feel free to creatively construct and publish whatever phony "scientific" evidence they wish to present to their government representatives as long as they don't mind spending the next 10 years of their life in solitary confinement writing research articles solely for the prison journal.

And so corporations and the wealthy have a much greater say on our college campuses and in our think tanks than years before. While opening up many avenues of enriching our elite academics, we should remain cautious that we do not lose the freedoms on campus that are so important not only for the education of our children, but the preservation of our democracy. Like all long-term strategic issues, the true pain will not be felt by Americans until it is too late to act.

Who Controls the Media?

The current great debate in media circles is whether the media in America has a liberal or a conservative bias. Some statistics say that 90% of on-air television news reporters vote Democratic. In addition, a number of best-selling books recently purport to expose this supposed liberal bias (see *The Savage Nation: Saving America from the Liberal Assault on Our Borders, Language, and Culture* by Michael Savage and *Bias: A CBS Insider Exposes How the Media Distort the News* by Bernard Goldberg).

At one time, most of the newspapers, radio stations and television networks in our country were owned by individuals, many potentially with a liberal bias. Their journalists grew up recognizing the critical importance that the media plays in acting as a watchdog of our government and the largest corporations in the country and they took great pride in confronting the establishment when good journalism dictated that they must.

There has been a tremendous sea change in the last 30 years in the make-up of the media. Almost all areas of the media industry have become dominated by corporations, and mostly by very large media conglomerates. Robert W. McChesney has documented these changes in his excellent book, *Rich Media, Poor Democracy* to demonstrate how dramatic and far reaching this consolidation has been.

McChesney names five conglomerates that dominate the media landscape:

AOL/Time Warner (WB)
Disney (ABC)
Viacom (CBS)
Rupert Murdoch's News Corporation (Fox)
Sony

They own and operate businesses in almost every arena of media, and as McChesney points out, they are eager to make bigger inroads into non-media businesses with product tie-ins and merchandise promotions. They own national television networks, television production facilities, television stations in local markets, cable TV programming and channels, newspapers, magazines, book publishers, radio stations, music businesses and movie studios and movie distribution businesses. And that is just in the U.S. They are very aggressively adding to their empires internationally. Right behind them are General Electric, which owns NBC and AT&T, which purchased TCI, the largest cable TV business in the country.

As McChesney demonstrates, corporate ownership and consolidation in each of the media business segments has grown tremendously. Television is dominated by the four networks -- ABC, NBC, CBS and Fox -- that are now all owned by very large corporations. News Corp. and its network, Fox, both are controlled by Rupert Murdoch, one of the most conservative businessmen in the world. In cable TV, seven firms control 75% of all cable channels and programming. In radio, traditionally a local medium, four giants control one-third of the total industry revenue of $13.6 billion, and much of the programming is produced nationally. Independent newspapers have been bought up by six major chains led by Gannett, Knight-Ridder, the Tribune Company and the New York Times Company. Hundreds of previously independent book publishers have been swallowed by seven dominant firms, while 80% of all books sold in the U.S. are retailed through a handful of national chains including Amazon.com, Borders and Barnes & Noble. The six largest film studios distribute 90% of all U.S. movies. Since Seagram purchased Polygram, the five largest music companies control 87% of the domestic music business. The jury is still out on attempts to concentrate ownership among Internet businesses, but each of the major conglomerates has made moves to try to wrest some control over what is presented as a rather uncontrollable medium. Time Warner merged with Internet giant AOL.

How is America's democracy threatened if media outlets are owned by a few, well-connected media conglomerates? Although the fact that all movies, music and entertainment programming are created and distributed by a few well-heeled corporations should give one pause, it is the collection and distribution of news that most affects a democracy. One could easily argue that our culture is as threatened as our democracy by the concentration of so many important art forms in a few corporate hands, but that is outside the purview of this book.

Immediate threats to our democracy are the primary concern here, and a fundamental requirement of any democracy is easy access to current and unbiased news. News about the country's government and how it is performing is critical, but also important is news about competing political parties, America's largest corporations, the way the outside world views America and its leaders and general reports about the welfare of the American people and their needs and desires. If the citizenry is unable to obtain such unbiased reporting in a timely fashion, people cannot be expected to be able to effectively judge the performance of their leaders or to monitor them properly. Any feedback the public gives its leaders is only as good as the information the public is given to react to.

So in this regard, a corporate roundup of the media businesses is most damaging if it adds a bias to the reporting of news in the country. Many people who enter the news profession, at least historically, may have had a somewhat liberal bias. The grand ambition of a great journalist, to find an earth-shattering story that exposes corruption or fraud at the highest levels of government or industry fits a renegade-type, non-establishment personality. But is this the kind of person the corporate media is hiring today? Are media outlets trying to find tough investigative journalists? Are they looking for the next Mike Wallace? No, many of the news anchors today are simply reading the evening news off cue cards, which is a far cry from the leadership roles Walter Cronkite and Edward R. Murrow played at CBS. The ideal hire at a network today is someone who will take orders from corporate headquarters and toe the line.

With regard to the content of the news, the new conservative corporate bias shows up not only in what is reported but also in what goes unreported. When was the last time you saw NBC run a news story critical of its parent, GE? Or has ABC ever done an expose on its corporate parent, Disney? A game theorist might argue that it is also unlikely that ABC would ever find fault with GE because GE might retaliate and find something critical of Disney to discuss on its NBC network. In fact, why would a corporate-owned news show be critical of any corporation? Aren't they all members of the same corporate family? Don't they all want the same things: low wages, open borders, free trade, less regulation and less taxation? When was the last time *60 Minutes* aired a real hard-hitting expose of a Fortune 500 company?

And how much coverage have you seen critical of defense spending or the weapons systems that are funded by it? Did you ever see a program that analyzed the suggested elimination of the inheritance tax and who might benefit? The standard line that small farmers and small business owners were the prime beneficiaries turned out to be blatantly false. It was the super-wealthy who were the recipients of one of the biggest tax giveaways in America's history.

Why were these stories not covered? Because there was not enough airtime given all the prime-time news specials that focused on welfare cheats, deadbeat dads, Medicare rip-offs, illegal immigrants, school lunch price increases and health care's rising costs. It seems the American government does not have the time or inclination to focus on these issues important to the common folk in America, but the networks have plenty of time to dedicate to using America's poorest citizens as scapegoats for why the government can't balance a federal budget. The entire sum of money spent on welfare for the families with dependent children program was $64 billion a year at its peak. This is about what the defense department spends every couple of months!

The mere fact that corporations are in the business of making money adds a distinct bias to news reporting. First of all, since the corporations' takeover, each of the news departments is now considered a profit center, whereas before it was understood each was providing a public service and typically ran at a loss. The immediate impact of this change in philosophy was that most of the networks had dramatic reductions in staffing. This meant fewer independent reporters covering and interpreting a news event and more sharing of news feeds between the networks. In his few and far between press conferences, President Bush regularly calls on the same journalists who he knows will ask safe questions, thus excluding questions from more controversial commentators.

More importantly, corporate ownership and a focus on profits changed the overall philosophy of the news departments. They now had to worry about ratings and viewership. It was as if the movie *Network* had suddenly come to life in all its splendor. News departments were being taken over by programming people, news was being treated like entertainment, and everything was as predicted in the movie except the fortuneteller doing the nightly weather report utilizing her crystal ball.

A dangerous precedent was established. A news show concerned with profits and ratings also had to be concerned with the quality of its interviews. The networks had to maintain access to the best talking heads, the biggest corporate executives and the highest office holders in the government. The news departments quickly learned that the way to maintain "access", their lifeblood, was to be nice to their interview guests. No hard-hitting questions, no accusations, no surprises -- in effect, no journalism. The nicer the interviewer, the higher the probability that he or she would continue to have access in the future and the greater the viewership and therefore the profitability.

Programming and even news content are steered by the demographics of the audience media executives want to attract. And what group has the best demographic profile for advertisers? The rich! So news became news that rich people wanted to see, and sometimes a bias slipped in to make that news more palatable to the rich. Cable news channels became constant ticker tapes, concerned solely with how the Dow Jones was doing that hour. It never occurred to anyone that the Dow Jones measured only investors' wealth and not the workers' well-being. Entire programs and even some entire cable channels became dedicated to reviewing stock market data and the companies that composed it. Economic reporting dwarfed all other types of reporting as if to say that if it didn't affect the Dow, it must not be much of a problem. When was the last time you saw a report on the national news about the inner cities, the rural poor, the concerns of our institutionalized elderly, complaints from prisons' inmates or the state of the poor in the developing world? It just doesn't affect the average stock portfolio. Americans are much more compassionate, generous and sympathetic than their television shows exhibit. But their target audience, the wealthiest Americans, may not be.

Obviously, a general pro-consumption and pro-growth message is important not only for pleasing corporate owners of the media, in general, but for selling ad time specifically. A different view is that the general trash the networks put out as entertainment, including reality programming, sitcoms and game shows, acts as the modern opiate of the masses. If the American public watches, it is hard to blame the networks. But networks have not acted as the guiding light to an enlightened new offering of culture and the arts on television.

The conservatives' dominance of radio is also interesting. Rush Limbaugh has done enormous damage to the spirit of free discourse with his polarizing and damning generalizations of the left and liberal politics. It is not just his philosophy that is extreme. He has made it acceptable to lie in defending one's positions. What can you say about talk show radio programming that features convicted felons Oliver North and G. Gordon Liddy as hosts of their own daily programs? And why do these talk show hosts attack the media as liberal? It allows them and their listeners to ignore any news that controverts their right-wing theories by denigrating the quality of the news source.

We might get more intelligent and unbiased programming by dedicating more resources to television's Public Broadcasting System (PBS) and radio's NPR, but these media outlets are not without fault. Because they feel they have to combat the conservative and corporate bias of the general for-profit media, they sometimes bend over backward and often suffer from extreme liberal bias. During the Iraq war, NPR scoured the country looking for guests who would be critical of the war effort. If the corporate bias of the mainstream media were straightened out, perhaps this reactive bias of the public media might correct itself.

Although there is no formal advertising on PBS, corporations may sponsor an entire program and receive on-air acknowledgement. PBS is probably less likely to air an expose of the huge subsidies going to agribusiness and ethanol production given that Archers Daniels Midland is one of its biggest sponsors. This problem too might go away if proper levels of public funding for public television and radio could be attained. Isn't it ironic that U.S. taxpayers pay to beam news free into repressive regimes, but do not adequately fund their own news efforts at home? Of course, the inadequate funding did not occur by mistake; it was a central element of the Republican congress's Contract with America in 1994. Originally, some die-hards wanted to cut funding altogether, but eventually they settled on leaving public broadcasting barely breathing on life support. The message got through. If public TV and radio maintained their liberal bias, further cuts were possible.

While public television and radio is in much better shape in Europe, there too it is coming under attack. Private media is launching an ambitious attempt to restrict public media's operations and to seek a cutback on its government funding. While limiting the for-profit activities of these public broadcasters may be appropriate, most likely conservative business owners will attempt to curtail their news operations. Europe only has to look to America to see how dangerous it is to silence the voice of public broadcasting.

So what damage has been done to America's democracy by the corporate takeover and consolidation of its media? An incalculable amount. How many wonderful books have never seen the light of day because they were not written by big-name establishment types or media personalities? What news is being censured by corporate entertainment executives? Who at these corporations is giving the green light to new movie scripts and what would they think of a documentary critical of American corporations? (Why did the movie *The Insider* open to such rave reviews, generate big initial box office numbers and then not spend the necessary advertising dollars to successfully roll out the picture to an even bigger audience?).

When corporations interfered with our news media, they damaged the fundamental fabric of America's democracy and its constitutional guarantees of individual freedom. The impact is already being felt, but its long-term effects can only be guessed. The news media are our eyes and ears to government, corporations and the world. If the images they provide are distorted, the damage is difficult to see and even more difficult to correct. While it is disturbing to see the problems inherent in our government, our businesses and our democracy, it is even more disturbing to realize that our media has been co-opted. It is hard to imagine how this message will ever reach a popular audience if our media opposes it.

Chapter 4

Written in January 2006

Selected Excerpts from *Sell Now! The End of the Housing Bubble*

Following are selected excerpts from "Sell Now! The End of the Housing Bubble", a book Talbott wrote and published in January 2006. The publisher was St. Martin's Griffin.

<u>Can We Predict Home Prices?</u>

If our banks and corporations are getting cozier with and closer to our government, this may be very bad for our economic outlook going forward, especially in regard to how we react to a possible bursting of the real estate bubble in this country. Maybe, American regulators like the Office of Federal Housing Enterprise Oversight (OFHEO) and the Federal Deposit Insurance Corporation (FDIC) and the Federal Reserve are not sufficiently independent from politics and corporate power to properly regulate the banks, Fannie Mae and Freddie Mac. Maybe, by lowering regulation we are increasing the odds of our ending up like Japan. Not only is the probability of experiencing an unsustainable economic bubble increased, but the odds of someone quickly and decisively stepping in to correct the situation as it deflates is much less. For the first time it is conceivable that our banks are being allowed to continue to add suspect mortgage loans to their balance sheets with the proviso that if they get in trouble the regulators will be very slow to step in and correct the situation. Unfortunately, if this is the case, the American economy will suffer tremendously in a housing downturn as trillions of bad real estate loans hang over the entire banking sector.

Even if you optimistically (and naïvely) believe our government is independent of political pressure brought on it by industry and the banks, the Fed may be very slow to force banks to recognize losses and thus push the problem out for years. In an attempt to protect some of our biggest banks and possibly avert a bank run on the entire system, The Fed may choose to punish the American economy for years as it struggles slowly out of the loan morass it created during this real estate bubble.

Evidence of a Bubble - More Evidence from the Cities of the World

The housing boom does indeed seem to be international. With the exception of Tokyo, Frankfurt and Toronto, the world's great cities have seen dramatic real price increases over the last 25 years.

The biggest percentage winners in this group are Dublin and Madrid. Both of these countries had explosive GDP growth over the period as they benefited from the formation of the European Union and opened their borders to foreign investment and trade. Historically, these cities' homes traded at a significant discount of 60 to 80 percent to homes in other European cities such as Amsterdam, Paris and Milan. Now, Dublin and Madrid have caught these cities in that their homes cost just about the same price. The question is no longer the appreciation these cities have experienced in the past, but rather whether they deserve to be valued as highly today as Paris and Milan. And it's not as if Paris and Milan were standing still during these years. Paris prices doubled and Milan's tripled in value.

Because prices have skyrocketed worldwide, it is much harder to argue that the cause is traceable to circumstances unique to the United States. For example, the popular argument that Mexican immigration, both legal and illegal, is partly responsible for the housing boom in the United States suffers when we look at the international data. Mexican immigration can't be blamed for price increases in Paris, Milan or London.

Can You Say "Conspiracy"?

Possibly the worst financial advice ever given to the American public was offered by Alan Greenspan in late 2004. Mr. Greenspan touted adjustable-rate mortgages (ARMs) to the public, saying, "American consumers might benefit if lenders provided greater mortgage product alternatives to the traditional fixed-rate mortgage." The most disturbing part of the advice is that we know Greenspan is smart enough to know better. Not only was it terrible advice, but Greenspan must have known it was bad advice before he gave it. Greenspan can be accused of many things, but being dumb is not one of them.

At best, Greenspan had ulterior motives besides simply helping the citizens he was supposed to serve. At worst, he was part of a grand conspiracy to aid the commercial banks and ignore the potential harm to the American public. If so, whose interests was he actually looking out for? Why would the Federal Reserve chairman do something so harmful to his own citizens? Who dreamed up this conspiracy?

At the time of Greenspan's terrible advice, adjustable-rate mortgages were growing tremendously in popularity with the American public. By early 2005, 35 percent of all new mortgages in the country were ARMs, and in California the percentage exceeded 70 percent. In addition to being floating-rate rather than fixed-rate instruments, many of these ARM deals combined other exotic features. Some did not require any principal repayment but rather required only interest payments. Others had initial periods of negative amortization; that is, the principal balance on the loan grew over time rather than declined.

Aggressive commercial banks and mortgage bankers were able to sell these instruments to homebuyers because they argued that it was silly to get a thirty-year-fixed-rate mortgage with a higher monthly mortgage payment if the buyer was only going to live in the new home for three to five years. What bankers particularly liked about the new mortgage instruments was that the new floating-rate or interest-only mortgage payment was lower than a standard self-amortizing thirty-year mortgage and so allowed potential homebuyers to qualify for ever-larger amounts of mortgage money. This was important because housing prices had reached such high levels in many communities that average folks could no longer qualify with the banks for the loans needed to buy homes under more conventional mortgage plans.

The homebuyers also bought into the logic. It made sense not to pay a premium to lock in rates for thirty years if they only planned to live in the house for five years. Moreover, experts in real estate, namely the broker and the mortgage banker were actively pushing the idea. This is why the Fed chairman's comments were so damaging. Surely, the homeowner could trust the chairman of the Federal Reserve to give unbiased advice on the matter. If Greenspan says it's good for me to get into ARMs, then it must be so. Isn't that one reason why we have government officials, to give us objective and unbiased expert advice? We look to the Food and Drug Administration to protect us from unsafe drugs. We look to building inspectors to expertly prevent buildings from collapsing and we should be able to look to the Federal Reserve and the FDIC to expertly protect the banking system from collapsing.

What is so terrible about ARMs that Greenspan knew but didn't tell homebuyers? First of all, long-term-thirty-year mortgage rates in 2005 were at a forty-year low. They had peaked at 16.5 percent back in 1981, but by 2005 were around 5.5 percent. This was an excellent opportunity for a homebuyer to lock in a very low rate for thirty years so that the mortgage payments could never vary in the future. If rates went even lower, you could always refinance. It is rare in finance that the public has such a valuable option given to it as the right to refinance if rates decline, but this is typical in thirty-year mortgages. By moving to floating rates, the homebuyer surrendered this option.

But the real travesty in people utilizing ARMs during this period is that it shifted all interest rate risk from the banks to the homeowners. Previously, market interest rates moving was a problem for the commercial banks, which were spending large amounts of money to hedge their interest rate exposure. Under ARM financings, the buyers had volunteered to absorb almost all future interest rate risk. The banks were able to sell the buyer on the idea by offering a short three- or five-year fixed-rate period during which the ARM interest rate did not reset. But after this, the ARM could float, and if market interest rates moved up considerably, then homeowners might see their scheduled monthly mortgage payments increase substantially, say 50 to 70 percent.

It is true that the homebuyer got a slightly lower rate by accepting a floating-rate deal, but because this financing package was being pushed on everyone, home prices immediately increased to offset any benefits resulting from the lower offered initial rate.

The more disturbing part of the story, and the part that Greenspan definitely knew but didn't tell the American public about, is that ARMs don't even make sense for those homebuyers who are only planning to stay put for three or five years. The broker's pitch to them was that they could always sell before the initial ARM's interest rate was scheduled to reset. What they, and Greenspan, forgot to tell the public was that if house prices had declined in the meantime, getting out of the house investment would be extremely difficult.

No one wanting to sell a home likes to see a down market for home prices. But the problem is multiplied for the ARM-financed homeowner. A homeowner with fixed-rate long-term debt has a locked-in monthly mortgage payment that cannot change in the future. If he doesn't like the housing market, he can always decide not to sell his home and continue to live in it and make his monthly mortgage payments. The ARM's homeowner has no such choice. Even if he believes a downturn in home prices might be temporary, he will be forced to sell his house into a weak market. The reason is that his mortgage payments will jump as soon as his initial fixed-rate period has expired if interest rates have increased. He will be between a rock and a hard place -- declining market values for his home and increasing monthly mortgage payments.

And here is the real dilemma. He is not alone. Tens of millions of ARM households may face the same decision -- sell into a down market or try to find a way to afford a much larger mortgage payment. Because so many will face this quandary at the same time, housing prices will grow even softer. Many people will sell into a weak housing market, not because they want to, but because they have to in order to avoid their ever-increasing mortgage payments. Such a selling stampede will drive housing prices even lower. And then the real carnage begins. Once housing prices are off 20 to 30 percent in some areas, many ARM homeowners will be financially underwater; that is, a home will be worth less in the market than the balance on the mortgage. And when that happens, the way out is not to sell but to allow the bank to foreclose and take possession of the home. Banks, too, will then begin selling repossessed real estate into the down market, joining the legion of ARM holders needing to sell and however many fixed-rate homeowners who have lost confidence in the housing market.

This is not idle speculation. More than $1 trillion of ARM mortgages are due to reset in 2007. And because interest rates are so low, their allowable increase in rate is a very large percentage of their total mortgage cost. Monthly payments could easily increase 50 to 70 percent. So the people who utilized ARM financings in order to stretch to afford their homes are exactly the ones who will suffer the greatest increases in rate. If you didn't qualify to buy a home utilizing a fixed-rate mortgage at 5.5 percent in 2005, you are not going to be able to afford to keep it when ARMs reset to 7 or 9 percent.

So again we face the same question. Why would Greenspan interfere in the markets to harm the average American worker? To see the answer clearly you must understand who Greenspan really works for.

It is true that the Federal Reserve chairman is appointed by the president, but the twelve regional Federal Reserve banks are controlled by our nation's commercial banks. Each reserve bank is managed by a board of nine directors, six of whom are nominated to serve by our commercial banks. And if you want to understand how they will decide any issue, just ask one simple question: What is in the commercial banks' best interest?

On many issues, what is good for the banking industry is good for Americans. But sometimes American workers' interests diverge from the banks', and it's unfortunate that the Federal Reserve chairman under those circumstances always seems to side with his banking friends. Keeping American wages low, under the guise of fighting inflation is one of those cases where Greenspan clearly puts the interest of his banking friends above the American workers. By keeping wages down, he helps American corporations become more profitable, and thus makes the bank's corporate lending portfolio all the more secure and profitable. To Greenspan, it is an unfortunate side effect that the American worker suffers so.

When it comes to housing and Greenspan's unforgivable bad advice on ARMs, it all becomes much clearer when one understands that Greenspan's primary allegiance is to the commercial banks and not to the public. By suggesting that Americans should take advantage of ARM financings, Greenspan should have recognized that he was harming American homebuyers. He was helping shift a potentially enormous problem from the commercial banks to the shoulders of the average workingman. In one piece of terrible advice, Greenspan was able to shift substantial future interest rate risk from his commercial banks and their balance sheets to American homeowners. He just forgot to disclose that he wasn't working on behalf of the American people; he was working to protect his banking cronies and prevent a possible future problem with the American banking system. Of course, the increasing utilization of ARM financings in the housing business has not reduced the risk to the banking system, it has worsened it. Shifting risk to individual homeowners does not free the banks from the credit risk they face of mortgage defaults, personal bankruptcies and foreclosures.

It is not just economic philosophy that drives Greenspan and the Bush administration to avoid the proper regulation of the banking sector and the mortgage industry. This administration has been corrupted by a system that allows our biggest banks and corporations to "buy off" our elected representatives through campaign contributions and lobbying efforts. Once the housing market collapses, we will all wonder why nothing was done sooner to prevent it. The answer, of course, is that most of our elected representatives in both parties, including our president, were being given a great deal of money not to do their jobs and not to protect the American people.

This pay for service is rampant throughout the federal government, but quite possibly the most damaging example is the way we regulate Fannie Mae and Freddie Mac. It was obvious to me when I wrote my first book in 2003 that these companies were too highly leveraged with debt and that too many of their business decisions were driven by an attempt to enrich their managements through profit-sharing schemes and generous stock options. Now, after they have announced tens of billions of dollars in unanticipated accounting adjustments and replaced their senior managements, they still are not receiving the government supervision they should. These two behemoths of the mortgage industry sit on trillions of dollars' worth of mortgages, and yet Congress has been very slow to properly regulate them. They enjoy an implied guarantee from the American taxpayer that saves them millions in borrowing costs and, yet, they feel no need to be regulated by Congress. It is the corruption of their multimillion-dollar lobbying effort that assures that congressmen look the other way, even after there has been every indication that there is a very serious problem. It would be sad enough if Fannie and Freddie were a major cause of a housing fiasco in the future that ended up harming many American families. It is inexcusable that our Congress has failed to act to better regulate these quasi-agencies having had the warnings that we have seen to date.

You don't have to believe in a grand conspiracy in order to realize that there is a housing bubble. But to those of you who depend on the government to protect your interests, you should be aware that times have changed. Your government is now controlled by the nation's biggest banks and corporations, which contribute to the election campaigns of elected officials and lobby them daily. Government's allegiance has shifted from concern for the people's business to profiting from it and allying themselves with big business. The housing crash will provide the evidence that people will point to in order to demonstrate with certainty that our government no longer puts their best interest at heart. It is sad that such pain to average Americans has to occur before people will act to reform our unrepresentative government, but Americans are slow to act, often doing nothing until after disasters explode.

I believe history will judge Greenspan and the current Congress and this administration much more harshly as caring much too deeply about bank and corporate profitability and knowingly creating an unsustainable housing bubble that threatened our very republic when it crashed. Everyone will certainly comprehend then that American homeowners took a beating during a housing crash that was the result of an unsustainable boom orchestrated and propped up by their government and big business, who were more interested in corporate profits than in the welfare of their fellow citizens.

The Real Culprit - Overly Aggressive Banks

So something very strange is happening here. Real housing prices are rising in nearly every single country of the world that is experiencing a decline in nominal interest rates and, yet, theory tells us that a change in nominal rates, with no change in underlying real rates, should not affect house prices. Is there a secondary effect that solves this conundrum?

To see what actually is happening, let's look at the problem from the perspective of the financing institution that funds home purchases, namely, the commercial banks. The primary tool commercial banks utilize in their determination of how much money to lend to a prospective home purchaser is the bank's qualifying formula. It has gotten more complicated with the advent of computers, but at its most basic it is still a first-year test of how comfortable the prospective buyer is in making his required mortgage payments given his current salary or income.

While a borrower is not required to spend all of the money he or she qualifies for, in the competitive world of house prices that is often exactly what ends up happening. Most of the formulas the banks utilize are some sort of ratio of your income in the first year to your total annual mortgage payments in the first year. And this is the problem. Mortgages are complex, sometimes thirty- to forty-year instruments. No adequate credit analysis can be reduced to a simple formula that focuses solely on the first year's coverage of mortgage interest, especially in a world of variable inflation rates. So when a bank officer talks about the percentage of pretax income that should go to a mortgage payment, or when she says you can afford a house equal to seven or eight times your current household income, please realize that this is a very simplistic analysis. Such an analysis can lead to very different results in differing interest rate and inflation environments.

These simple first-year-ratio bank qualifying formulas may be behind the entire worldwide bubble in residential real estate prices. Imagine that the entire world's real estate may be overvalued because bankers are all using similar shorthand analyses to determine appropriate lending amounts and those analyses may have fatal flaws.

Mortgage bankers are proud of the panoply of mortgage products they have introduced in the last ten years. Interest-only mortgages, negative amortization loans, multiple option loans have all gained tremendous acceptance in the market and now represent some 35 percent of newly issued nationally. The sole purpose of such plans that lower the initial mortgage payment is to allow cash-tight buyers to stretch on the price they can pay for a home. Buyers who qualify for $400,000 of lending under a conventional mortgage may qualify for $500,000 under a floating-rate deal or even $550,000 if they defer paying back principal or if they let the loan balance grow over time.

If we are right that the availability of easy money from bankers is a primary reason for the real estate housing boom, then we ought to be able to find a way to test this supposition. If bankers in misapplying overly generous qualifying formulas and aggressively offering zero-down, floating-rate, interest-only deals, are saturating the housing markets with money, then we ought to be able to measure their effect statistically. Because bank money is the predominant source of financing for a home purchase, we would expect to see higher home prices in areas in which bankers are more active and lend more aggressively. For these purposes, we have removed the homebuyer from the equation and assumed that he spends nearly every dollar that he qualifies for. Let us see if we can establish a relationship between the location of the most aggressive commercial bankers and where housing prices have increased the fastest.

We have seen that house prices in the wealthiest communities and cities in America have appreciated the most over the last ten years. This is most evident in the analysis of housing P/E expansions by city. Is there a reason to suggest that overly aggressive bankers might be the cause of this phenomenon? Why would bankers tend to be more active in the mortgage markets of wealthy communities than other neighborhoods in general?

With some 99.5 percent statistical confidence, the wealthiest communities five years ago in terms of levels of housing prices have experienced the highest home price appreciation since then. One plausible explanation of this data is that these cities have had a disproportionate level of involvement by the overly aggressive banks through jumbo mortgages and their cheaply available bank funds have been the driving force behind the recent home price appreciation.

In addition to examining which cities utilized the greatest percentage of jumbo mortgages and, therefore, had the greatest involvement of aggressive private bankers, I also examined which cities in America were the most aggressive in utilizing more exotic financing tools such as interest-only mortgages. If banks' aggressiveness is a major contributor to housing price increases across the county, one would expect to find that those cities that had utilized the greatest percentage of interest-only loans also have had the greatest price appreciation in homes. The percentage of interest-only loans in each city becomes a proxy of how aggressive bankers are in that region.

As expected, the statistical analysis at a 95 percent confidence level demonstrates that those cities that made the greatest use of interest-only mortgages also experienced the greatest price appreciation over the five-year period. It appears that those communities that were exposed to the greatest percentage of aggressive private bank lending indeed experienced the greatest degree of home price appreciation.

The Desire for Status

If we currently have a bubble in real estate, those homebuyers who are overpaying for homes and those banks that are aggressively financing them have not paid yet for their mistakes. In fact, they have been rewarded. They have enjoyed ever-greater profits riding what is an unsustainable wave of ever-increasing home prices. Is there some other component or benefit that a person might garner by purchasing a home?

My answer is that individuals' quest for status might explain it all. There are goods that economists have often referred to as luxury or status goods because some people feel compelled to buy more of them even as their price increases. People seem to have identified diamonds and jewels and motor yachts as products that they don't mind paying exorbitant prices for because that is part of the status game. The fact that the price is ridiculous signals that the owner has plenty of money, power and status, and the high price also prevents status imposters from making the same acquisition. Under this model, the higher the price, the more exclusive the purchase and the greater status achieved. The fact that status demand might increase as prices increase make the product more "exclusive" meaning that traditional economic supply and demand analysis does not apply.

While people are familiar with $10,000 designer dresses and million-dollar automobiles, we usually don't think of housing as a status item. But what started out as simple shelter, as recently as our parents' generation, now often has a status element attached to it reflected in its size, its amenities and the neighborhood and city in which it is located. If you doubt this, think about a home purchase you have made or heard of recently. Was the home purchased because it had an adequate number of bedrooms for the people living there? Was it highly valued because it was in the right school district? Or was a high price paid because it was in the right community or had the right zip code? Did the real estate agent point out celebrities that lived nearby? Did you check out the view instead of the water pressure in the shower? What was the real reason for insisting on a five-acre plot instead of one acre? Were you more concerned that you would like the place or that your guests would?

I originally thought of the idea of the importance of status to housing when I reviewed the list of cities worldwide that were experiencing the fastest appreciation in housing prices and the greatest divergence from rental values. Miami Beach. San Francisco. New York City. Paris. London. Aspen. Nice. Las Vegas. Madrid. Saint-Tropez. These are some of the wealthiest and most exclusive communities in the world. Remember, this is not a list of the most expensive places to live; rather it is a list of cities in which home prices have appreciated the most recently. I started to investigate whether the result would be limited to only our richest cities.

The cities with the fastest appreciating home prices are those in which residents put an unusually high degree of emphasis on status. The anonymity of large cities pushes people to find ways to differentiate themselves, and these large cities seem to attract ambitious people for which success and status is extremely important.

It also partially explains why the cities and neighborhoods with the most expensive houses have witnessed the greatest appreciation recently. The whole idea of status is exclusivity. If a community isn't exclusive, it can't confer status. And the best way to create exclusivity is to raise prices. Only the rich need apply.

It turns out my theory of status also dovetails quite well with Glaeser's and Gyourko's work on restrictive zoning and housing prices. The communities with the greatest zoning restrictions are trying to create exclusivity, the key to status.

But that doesn't explain why purchase prices in these exclusive cities have gotten so out of line with rentals. Or does it? If you rent in one of these wealthy communities, are you really part of the community? Do renters get invited to join the golf club? Maybe the disparity between rents and purchase costs is the best indicator that status is indeed playing a large part in setting prices in these exclusive communities.

And a status theory of housing values explains why the most costly homes and the greatest price appreciation has occurred in our major cities and not out in rural areas. What good is buying a luxury home if no one is there to see you in it? Just as an unobserved tree falling in the forest makes no noise, a big beautiful home out in the lonely woods does little to increase status. The key to appreciating status is to have an audience -- and there is no bigger audience than that of our major cities and the playgrounds of our wealthiest residents.

Finally, status can also explain the international component of the housing boom, as status seeking is not an exclusively American pastime. Sure enough, the cities that have seen the fastest escalation in housing prices worldwide are the homes of the rich and famous. And within each city, the neighborhoods that have the fastest-growing prices are the ritziest and priciest.

It seems reasonable to assume that if two condominium apartments on the top two floors in a high-rise building share exactly the same floor plan, the same views, and the same roof decks and access, then any price premium paid for the penthouse as opposed to the floor directly under it would have to be chalked up to status. And we know that this price difference can be very large, often representing 20 to 50 percent of the total value of the penthouse. Penthouses are ideal status goods because no one can have a higher condo in a building than the penthouse.

There is much anecdotal evidence that people will pay a premium to live right on the coast as opposed to being a block from the ocean. Here the view and beach access is important, but it is also very important to be able to show your friends that you can't get closer to the water without a snorkel. Perhaps this is why coastline properties have recently risen in price the most. I think there is also a status component to paying high prices for condos with spectacular views, as I believe many owners rarely take advantage of the view themselves but always point it out when their status-determining friends come to visit.

If I am right that status drives home prices, then in order for real house prices to have increased in price exponentially recently there must have been an increase in the importance of status over time. If we remember our parents' lives and where they chose to retire, and compared it to our own and our friends' status-conscious lives, I think there is a solid argument that status is not only more important today than it used to be, but that its importance is growing.

Nominal Price Appreciation of a Number of Selected Status Goods Compared to Median Existing Home Price Appreciation 1976-2004

Status Good and Price Increase '76 to '04

Groton - 8.5x
Harvard - 6.8x
Opera/Met - 9.8x
Dom Perignon - 4.8x
Dinner/Paris - 9.7x
Hotel/NYC - 3.7x
Yacht/75' - 21.0x
Sailboat/68' - 10.1x
Learjet - 4.6x
Helicopter - 6.9x
Rolls-Royce - 8.7x

CPI Index - 3.3x
Home Prices - 5.5x

Source of Data: Forbes Magazine, Analysis: Author

Home prices increasing fivefold over this thirty-year period no longer look unusual when compared to other goods status seekers seek. Startlingly, seventy-five-foot yachts have increased 21 times in value in thirty years. Certainly, they are much better equipped today, so the price multiple overstates their true economic appreciation. But it now takes a 400-foot yacht to grab the attention of the world yachting community, and some yacht clubs won't even take boats as small as seventy-five feet. The biggest personal yachts today cost over $250 million to build, which puts the $4.5 million Hatteras in Table 9.2 to shame. Therefore, maybe this table understates the appreciation of true status in those categories.

Clearly, if people have a sudden moral awakening and realize that life has more to offer than a never-ending race to consume more than a neighbor, housing prices in the ritziest neighborhoods could come under pressure. But we don't have to wait for such a moral epiphany. Because paying big prices for houses solely to acquire status is economically unproductive, buyers will not be able to recoup their investments in rental incomes. Banks will eventually pull the plug on this type of lottery-like status seeking, so the housing market will crash regardless of whether status seekers mend their ways. And many of the most stretched status seekers will exhaust their incomes long before they ever become satisfied with the size of their homes or the look of their neighbors.

The Morning After

There are very strong indications that the global housing boom is finally over. Industry experts have tried to predict what the post-boom era will look like. Their predictions are as unreasonably optimistic as they were during the boom. These experts suggest that if there is a decline, it will be regional in nature, only affect the most overpriced cities, not unduly impact the U.S. economy and will be more of a soft landing than a total collapse. They universally agree that home prices will continue to grow at 4 to 6 percent in the future.

That is one scenario. But that is not the most likely scenario. Prices have gone up too much in too many areas for there not to be a major correction that will be national, or possibly global, and that will have a very meaningful impact on the world economy.

Even those who argue that the impact will be limited to the most overpriced cities fail to see that these very much overpriced cities are also our largest cities with the highest aggregate values of real estate. The twenty-two most overpriced cities represent more than 40 percent of the total value of all residential real estate in the country. Even if a housing correction were somehow magically constrained within their city limits, the negative wealth effects would be felt countrywide.

So the first fallout from a pricing decline in the wealthiest neighborhoods will be a reduction of new home construction and sales on the periphery of these neighborhoods and cities. Secondly, while the wealthy may have additional resources that prevent them from losing their homes to foreclosure in a downturn, those status-seeking young couples trying desperately to keep up with the Joneses by buying homes beyond their means will really get squeezed. Many million-dollar homes will face foreclosure as overleveraged owners realize that the economics work better with the property dead rather than alive. People will understand that they can't afford high mortgage payments during tough economic times and will come to realize that in a world of depressed real estate prices it makes more sense to default to the bank than sell the property and realize less than the balance on the mortgage.

So wealthy neighborhoods will suffer losses as those stretched are forced to default and banks repossess and cause forced auctions in the market. The rich will suffer equally on paper but will most likely avoid losing their homes, as they will continue to make their mortgage payments, even if they have to eat into their savings to do it.

The secondary impact from the biggest and wealthiest cities undergoing a correction may be even larger than the damage in the wealthy enclaves themselves. Real estate downturns always hit harder in the more middle-class neighborhoods because it is these people who are dependent on a healthy economy and job outlook to make their monthly mortgage payments. Look at Los Angeles and San Diego. The real fallout from a housing correction will be felt hours away in San Bernardino and Riverside as many middle-income residents of San Diego and LA look miles inland in search of more reasonably-priced homes. The lucky ones reinvested the profits they made in the sale of their LA and San Diego homes, and so their losses will likely be limited to giving back the paper profits they made during the boom. But many will suffer real losses when housing collapses in these inland areas because it no longer will be necessary to commute hundreds of miles in order to work in San Diego or Los Angeles.

There is another secondary effect that will cause even greater damage than the initial shock felt by the overpriced wealthy epicenter of the coming housing collapse. The economy will take a very big hit from the housing collapse, and the fallout from the economic retrenchment will hit our more modest communities the hardest. Although the Midwest and the interior states have not enjoyed anywhere near the home price appreciation of our coastal cities, they will still face severe housing price risk as the weakened economy shakes through their towns. These are poorer communities to begin with. Many have been losing population, they are not as plugged into the global economy as our coastal cities are and their manufacturing prowess has been in a long decline. Once accelerated job losses associated with the end of the housing boom hit these more traditional American towns, their home prices will drop violently downward. A $125,000 house in the Midwest that has appreciated $20,000 in the last nine years has as big a percentage risk of a decline in price as a three million dollar home in Malibu. When moderate income cities get hit with a bad economy and a weak housing market, people miss mortgage payments, banks foreclose, and then prices really fall. As I said earlier, if home prices have not grown tremendously in your town because of lots of new home construction, this increase in supply may act to severely depress prices once the artificial demand is lessened and the easy mortgage money dries up. Houses do not have to go up in price in order to come down. The prices of many homes in the Midwest will end up lower than they were before the boom.

How big will the impact of a housing retrenchment be on the general economy? Enormous! People have mistakenly tried to compare a national housing collapse to a bear market in stocks. There is no comparison. The U.S. stock market in total is worth some $15 trillion. Residential real estate in America is now valued at more than $20 trillion. And that is not the only difference. More than 75 percent of all U.S. stocks held by individuals are held by the richest 10 percent of the population. Nearly 70 percent of Americans own their own homes. A housing decline will be felt much more broadly.

While historically stocks are more volatile in price than housing, housing is typically purchased with significantly more debt leverage. A typical home is purchased with 80 to 90 percent debt. The total margin debt relative to the value of all stocks is less than 5 percent. This means that the net effect on investor wealth is five to ten times higher for a similar housing price percentage decline as compared to a stock decline.

Imagine a stock market decline so substantial that 50 to 100 percent of many investors' net worth evaporated. It has never happened, not even during the market crash of 1929. If housing declines in price by 30 percent, which is simply a return to where prices were in many cities just two years ago, many people would lose most of all of their net worth. Economists talk about the wealth effects when homeowners feel "slightly" poorer if housing prices adjust a little. Nobody is talking about the correct magnitudes of this possible disaster. Prices could easily return to where they were seven to nine years ago. For those big cities that have seen the biggest home price appreciations recently, this would mean a decline in home values of approximately 50 to 60 percent. Such a large price adjustment would wipe out almost everyone's total home equity. It is silly to talk about what the wealth effect on GDP might be in such a scenario since lots of people wouldn't have any wealth left to talk about.

It is important to highlight these worst-case scenarios because most of the media discussion to date about the ramifications of a housing decline has been driven by very optimistic scenarios that involve slight price downturns and predictions of soft landings or pauses in a continually increasing market. If we begin to understand the risks involved on the downside, we will begin to dedicate the resources and attention we need to try to avert a real disaster.

The major impact of an adjustment in housing prices on the economy is not going to be due to the wealth effect. It will result from the simple fact that our economy for at least five years has been built on only two foundations, the housing market and government (mainly military) spending.

I firmly believe that had it not been for the housing boom, the U.S. economy would have contracted over the last five years. Economists generally underestimate both the impact of the housing boom on GDP growth historically and the effect a housing price decline might have.

The first and obvious economic impact is that about a million real estate brokers who have been chasing 6 percent commissions on million-dollar homes with lottery-like enthusiasm will immediately become unemployed. Next, there are at least a million more people who work as mortgage bankers, appraisers, title lawyers, commercial bankers and mortgage packagers who are also going to have to dust off their résumés.

It is hard to estimate percentages, but one would expect the mortgage business to slow by at least 60 percent in a downturn and the brokerage business to fall by a similar amount. If prices drop 30 percent and volume of sales is off by half, real estate commissions paid will be reduced by 65 percent, and that assumes that the realtors' fee commission schedule holds at current percentages.

The economic impact of a housing price decline is not limited to the real estate agent and mortgage community. The next business that will dry up is the renovation business. Owners will have no motivation to renovate the kitchen or add another bathroom if their home is worth less than they paid for it. New home construction will also almost cease. In effect, homebuilders have built out any land they can find that they can make a profit on at the boom level of prices. If prices adjust downward 30 to 40 percent, there will be no more projects that make sense.

The construction industry, the home renovation industry, the banking industry and the real estate industry are four of the largest industries in America. Layoffs in these industries will be significant enough to cause a major recession. But, unfortunately, the story is not over.

Free market economies suffer ripple effects. When Suzie Realtor gets laid off, she buys fewer groceries, attends fewer movies, buys fewer dresses, takes fewer vacations, buys a new car less frequently and eats out less often. Thus, the economic impact is not going to be limited to a few of our largest industries. The pullback in consumption from those who face reduced salaries and layoffs in the housing industry will pull other healthy industries down with them. Layoffs will spread, and the economy will begin a serious contraction.

We have already seen that the housing bubble is not limited to the United States. Other countries facing bubble-like real estate prices will begin their contraction. Because the United Sates is such a driving force of the world's total overall consumption, a recession here is sure to spread globally. There is no world power that can replace the purchasing power that might evaporate in the United States. So the recession that starts here will be the force that ends up deflating the housing bubbles worldwide. Global recessions will result. No country will escape, as even developing countries that have no housing bubble will suffer mightily once domestic economic growth turns negative. The first rule of developing country economics is no U.S. growth, no U.S. consumer demand, no developing country growth. Thanks to globalization we are all in this together.

If you are squeamish perhaps you should stop reading here, for I have not told you the worst part. Remember that significant amount of debt leverage that homeowners have on their homes that magnifies any housing price decline and increases the impact on homeowners' equity? There is a counterpart to that debt that suffers as well. We cannot forget the banks, Fannie Mae, Freddie Mac and the other institutional holders of all the mortgage paper we have created. Because banks, as we have seen, have become so aggressive in their mortgage lending, much of this mortgage paper will be fairly worthless when home prices decline, at least as a tradable financing instrument. Its new value will be whatever a bank can realize from a quick sale of the house in foreclosure. But if a mortgage is written on 90 percent of the value of a house and the home price declines 30 percent, the bank will be lucky to recoup half of its invested funds through foreclosure and a forced property sale.

Fannie Mae and Freddie Mac are leveraged over 100 to 1 in aggregate (that is, their real assets only cover 1 percent of their loans), so if only 2 percent of their portfolio experienced 50 percent credit losses, they would be technically out of business. The taxpayers would have to pick up the bill under their implied guarantees, a tab that could easily run as much as 20 percent of their total assets, or approximately $500 billion.

And because 40 percent of the total assets of commercial banks are residential mortgages and real estate holdings, a decline of only 12 percent in the price of their entire portfolios of mortgages and owned real estate assets would wipe out their total bank equity, which is typically about 5 percent of their total assets.

Worse, banks don't actually have to lose money before the real threat is realized. The real threat is the loss of confidence of depositors in the banking system. If depositors believe there is a chance that their deposits will be impaired, they can withdraw them. Of course, because banks leverage deposits, they have only about 5 percent in cash on hand at any time to repay all the depositors. The rest is in illiquid longer-term assets like mortgages and business loans. If people decide they want to withdraw their money from the bank all at one time, a bank run can start. The federal government has adequate means to prevent a bank run on any one institution, but it does not have the liquidity to save all the banks. Because this would be the first national housing crash, and because almost all banks hold a significant amount of their assets in mortgages, the federal government would have great difficulty guaranteeing all the depositors' funds. We are talking trillions of dollars in deposits that might want to walk out the door in any one day. Even the U.S. government could not borrow that sum quickly, especially when a bank-run rumor was widespread.

A $5 trillion decline in the value of residential real estate in America, or a worldwide housing price decline of $15 trillion, is almost impossible to handle and maintain the stability of the banking system. Very few governments are large enough or have adequate reserves to handle these numbers. The entire GDP of all the advanced countries of the world is just $30 trillion. As we saw in the Great Depression, when the world loses its confidence in business and government's ability to properly regulate it; the results can be tragic. It took almost thirteen years for the United States to fully recover from the crash of 1929. Free market economies require the confidence of consumers, workers, producers, lenders and savers that contracts will be honored and banking and monetary systems will be stable. When we lose the ability of our government to properly regulate free enterprise, we run the risk of losing our country and our freedom.

The following shows just how much home prices must decline in real terms just to get them back to their 1997 levels, before most of this nonsense started. The 1997 prices have been adjusted at the general inflation rate so they are now reported in constant 2005 dollars.

Real Price Decline Required to Return to 1997 Price Level

Mean Decline   -24.7%
Median Decline   -18.0%
Top 40 Cities Decline   -47.2%

Source of Analysis: Author

To see how this analysis applies to your own home, you need to estimate what its market value was in 1997. Then multiply this value by 1.212 to convert the 1997 value into 2005 constant dollars and adjust for general inflation. This is the price level your home may return to in more normal times over the next five to seven years.

If my thesis is correct, 1997 was a time before most of the banks in the mortgage business went crazy. It predated their use of ARMs and interest-only loans to stretch the amount of money they would lend. It also predated the significant decline in nominal interest rates that has occurred since.

But since 1997, lending amounts have skyrocketed, mostly due to the misapplication of a bank qualifying formula that confused nominal rates with real interest rates. By returning to 1997 housing price levels we are returning to a time before banks went crazy with exotic mortgages and the application of overly aggressive bank qualifying formulas.

Santa Barbara is the most overpriced town in America according to this analysis. Santa Barbara's home prices are being supported by the unusually high underlying land values. People do not pay a huge premium for land in Santa Barbara because it is some kind of ticket to high incomes. You don't need to live in Santa Barbara to work in Los Angeles. Residents only pay it because they value Santa Barbara's amenities -- its weather and its coastline and its views. And I believe they pay a significant status premium because they like Santa Barbara's exclusivity.

Even after the easy bank money departs the system and some rationality returns to the pricing of homes, Santa Barbara will still trade at a significant premium to other homes in the country. But this premium will always be suspect because it will have nothing to do with providing adequate shelter for one's family but rather reflect a culture of consumerism and indulgence and status seeking. People who pay millions to live in Santa Barbara are not investing. It is pure consumption. They are treating themselves to amenities that they and their family can enjoy. And in the case of the artificial status they create by paying so much for simple housing, they had better get great personal satisfaction from it because it is not doing anything productive for the rest of humanity.

A nice test of this prediction is to compare these results with our analysis of how overvalued these cities' real estate markets are relative to underlying rental markets. Remember, average housing P/E multiples seemed to have expanded 47 percent or so, inexplicably, given that real interest rates did not change substantially during the period. This ties in quite well with the current analysis, as prices that had appreciated 47 percent too fast would have to decline 32 percent in the future to get back in line with historical average P/E levels.

How can you analyze your personal situation to see if it makes sense to sell now? You should sell any investment or vacation properties that are over $200,000 in value, and for lesser-valued properties, a tough cost-benefit analysis should be run. If your primary residence is worth at least $330,000, and you can sell your home and pocket tax-free profits you should most definitely do it. Real profits or avoided losses should represent at least $100,000 for this size house, and it could mean millions in savings for much higher-priced homes. This is real money that will become even more valuable to you as we enter a tight money period associated with a bank pullback. You should do it to have investment monies to utilize elsewhere, but mostly you should do it to get money out of what is a dead asset, your home. Don't think you have to put the profits in the stock market. If you are interested in status, you can pool your winnings with a couple of friends and open the hottest restaurant in town.

It is much harder for people with $150,000 to $330,000 homes to decide what to do because of large transaction costs. I would think that it doesn't make sense for people with homes worth less than $150,000 to do anything but ride out the storm the best they can. Clearly, they will want to get their leverage in order and fix any floating interest rates on their debts, but selling probably does not net them much in total pickup value.

In conclusion, it would be natural for a homeowner to believe that we will never return to 1997 price levels for residential real estate. Even though that is our country's history with real estate prices, and is exactly Japan's experience, it is hard to admit that we might give back all the paper profits we have earned over the last nine years. Surely, the world is different today. On that, you will get no argument. But in meaningful, fundamental ways that impact home prices, namely, in construction costs, average incomes, rental incomes available and physical layouts like length of coastlines or available views, there has been very little real change over the period. The changes that have occurred -- greater emphasis on consumption and status, overly aggressive bank lending, temporary constraints on new building or buyers' beliefs that prices will always increase in the future -- all are really quite temporary in nature. It is the nature of markets that they go up and down. At times they get carried away with short-term and unexpected increases in demand, but they always return to a price level that properly reflects the key fundamentals of price determination.

Government officials hide behind the excuse that the free market will take care of everything if we just allow it to operate. But the housing market is not a free market. There is nothing free market about granting Fannie Mae and Freddie Mac implied guarantees that their debt will be backed by the American taxpayer if there is a problem in the future. There is nothing free market about banks extending trillions of dollars of mortgage loans, taking huge upfront fees, and then selling the assets upstream to Fannie and Freddie. There is nothing free market about buyers bidding for houses with other people's money and no money of their own at risk. There is nothing free market about banks collecting up-front fees on such long-lived assets as home mortgages without any concern for their long-term viability. There is nothing free market about interest rates being depressed temporarily because the world's richest democracy needs to borrow money from the world's largest Communist dictatorship to make ends meet.

As usual, it will be the unsuspecting public that will be left holding the bag when all this gets sorted out. The taxpayer will have to honor Fannie Mae and Freddie Mac debt commitments. The taxpayer will absorb the cost of cleaning up the real estate and mortgage industry. The public will absorb the trillions of dollars of cost of bailing out the commercial banks that get in trouble with their mortgage portfolios. And the public will suffer layoffs and wage hits as they weather the recession or depression that will result when these major housing-related industries plummet, taking the entire economy with them. And during all this pain, the public will wrestle with losing their homes to foreclosure when many will find their mortgage balances far exceed their homes' depressed true market values.

While the highest priced and wealthiest cities of the world are at greatest risk of a correction in home prices, the damage will not stop there. Those most at risk are the people who have stretched their earnings to maximize their leverage and have paid far more for properties than they can afford. But the middle class across the country will also suffer. As foreclosures increase, banks will pull back in their lending, home prices will drop, and the economy will tank. This will lead to layoffs in middle-class towns and more foreclosures and still lower home prices. As is typical, the middle class will suffer the most even though they were not the biggest offenders when it came to paying high prices for homes. A weakened economy will drive all home prices down, and the middle class will suffer the majority of the job layoffs. This will lead to the loss of their homes in many cities that have not participated in the housing boom to date.

America has become a much less democratic, egalitarian, equal-opportunity place to live over the last thirty years. It is almost impossible for an incumbent in Congress to lose a reelection bid given the way congressional districts have been gerrymandered. Presidential candidates of both parties seem to represent the interests of the wealthy and the incorporated who can afford to give them large campaign contributions. Our best private schools are reserved for families that can afford tens of thousands of dollars in tuition while our public schools are in disarray. And for the first time in America, privilege and social position will become inheritable as Congress acts to permanently eliminate the inheritance tax.

America is literally dividing into two countries, wealthy America and poor and middle-class America. Entire communities like San Diego and San Francisco and Manhattan are reserved for the wealthiest. Americans having more moderate incomes are being forced to find homes elsewhere. Low-income Mexican immigration provides a steady stream of cheap labor, but destroys our unions and wage structure in the meantime. Globalization puts our poorest in direct competition for jobs and wages with the world's poorest, many of whom live in repressive dictatorships with no guarantee of basic human rights. We are quickly becoming a country of haves and have-nots, with the number of Americans living in poverty increasing for the fourth straight year. The American public never reacted when they watched their precious democracy slowly evaporate before the will of big donors and big business. Now, the coming housing crash is the result of allowing our government to work on behalf of our biggest banks and corporations rather than our people. Maybe, just maybe, people will realize that government must be responsive to its people; that free markets cannot operate without proper regulation, and that elected representatives' sole allegiance must be to the people. The people, hopefully, will finally stand up and act to save their republic and assure that the suffering caused by the end of the housing bubble is never allowed to occur on our shores again.

Chapter 5

Written in July 2008

Selected Excerpts from *Obamanomics*

Following are selected excerpts from "Obamanomics", a book Talbott wrote and published in July 2008. The publisher was Seven Stories Press.

Cooperation is the Key

   Listed below is my attempt to generate a list of the 25 Greatest Threats to Our Prosperity, ranked by a hypothetical worst case cost, which is nothing more than a back of the envelope guesstimate of what the potential total cost might be over time. While certain to be highly controversial, it is meant as only an order of magnitude expression of potential costs over time, knowing that others might disagree with the ranking and the cost estimates. Part of the reason for creating such a table is to encourage such disagreement and debate that is healthy and productive. If we can't even decide which are the biggest problems facing us, how can we be expected to prioritize them or attack them and find solutions? Please realize these hypothetical costs are presented in trillions of dollars, so all threats on these pages are meaningful and quite large. The table also makes the point nicely that all of these issues are, in fact, economic as they all have real dollar costs associated with them.

25 GREATEST THREATS TO OUR PROSPERITY

Name of Threat and Potential NPV Cost in Trillions

1 - World Poverty - $100
2 - Global Warming - $60
3 – Globalization - $60
4 – Corruption - $50
5 - Human Rights - $50
6 – Population - $50
7 – Education - $50

8 - Trade w/China - $50
9 – Aging - $40
10 - Energy Policy - $40
11 - Workers' Rights - $40
12 – Environment - $20
13 - Animal Rights - $20
14 - Health Issues - $20
15 – Racism - $20
16 – Imperialism - $20
17 - Deficits and Debt - $15
18 – Housing - $10
19 - Corporate Media - $10
20 – War - $10
21 – Fundamentalism - $10
22 – Crime - $10
23 - Tobacco Use - $10
24 – WMD - $10
25 – Terrorism - $5

One might be surprised to see both weapons of mass destruction (WMD) and terrorism ranked as low as twenty-fourth and twenty-fifth as potential threats in this table given their constant exposure in the media as very serious threats to the peace and stability of the world. In the table, this exposure to WMD and terrorism is quantified at $10 trillion and $5 trillion, respectively, which in absolute dollars is highly significant. The fact that the other threats listed in the table have even larger costs assigned to them should not diminish the public's perceived risk of WMD and terrorism, but should provide a valuable benchmark by which the sheer magnitude of the danger inherent in the other listed threats can be judged.

Werner Hans Erhard, the founder of EST training, formally launched in 1977 an attempt to end world hunger by the year 2000 called the Hunger Project, Erhard was drawn to the fact that there was enough food grown on the planet each year to feed everyone, but that many still starved. His solution was that the world's hunger problem could simply be willed away if enough people took responsibility for realizing the problem was conquerable and dedicated themselves to attacking it.

I don't want to be placed in the company of people like Erhard, who started life as Jack Rosenberg, a used car and encyclopedia salesman, and has been widely reported to be a fraud and a huckster, but it is just possible he was onto something. No, hunger cannot be willed away. It exists not because of inadequate foodstuffs, but because the world's poor have inadequate incomes to buy sufficient food to feed their families. International aid programs that depend on grants and food distribution ease suffering in the short term, but do little to address the fundamental problem that many of the world's poor are working hard, but just not producing and earning sufficiently to provide for their families.

But, as Erhard implies, the key to the solution to many of the complex problems we face today may lie within ourselves and blame should not so easily be shifted to our corrupt governments or our greedy capitalist enterprises. We cannot just will away these problems, but a healthy shift in the focus of our energy, efforts and motivations toward cooperation might be the critical element necessary to generate effective solutions. If you trace these greatest threats back to their root causes, you see that, yes, corporate greed and politicians' ruthlessness contribute, but ultimately it is the people who have decided which course they want their governments to pursue and what objectives they wish society to focus on.

It turns out that one thing is needed to solve each of these important problems, greater global cooperation. Individual effort won't do it. The problems are too large and too complex. A single citizen who tries on his own to work toward a solution will either see very little benefit or, in fact, may face a competitive disadvantage relative to those who ignore the problems. In the parlance of economics, all of these are collective action problems because individuals acting in their own self-interest will arrive at an equilibrium solution that is not as good for all than if the participants had cooperated and acted together.

These problems have not been solved because 1) the free market's individual participants were not motivated monetarily to find a cooperative solution, 2) the U.S. government was too busy taking industry's money to focus on issues of importance to its people, 3) all governments are poorly organized to begin with as they have no quantitative measurement system to reward and punish, and 4) many of these problems involve international cooperation beyond the scope of any one people's government.

As problems reach national and international scope in size, it is very difficult for cooperation to occur without democracy. A country's citizens can't just call a national town hall meeting to discuss their concerns. They must have in place some method of having the collective voice of the people reach their elected representatives and be heard. This is why a free press, civil liberties and elections are so important, not only for democracy, but for any cooperative effort among citizens. Cooperation is a necessary ingredient for successful democracy, but for large scale countries and regions, democratic institutions are also essential to encouraging cooperative solutions to problems. No other societal organizing principle other than democracy can assure that the people are deciding issues most important to them, and without democratic institutions there can be no broad cooperation among citizens spread over vast distances.

While we can hope that mankind will become more compassionate and show greater concern for the welfare of others over time, realistically it must be said that the primary reason that people cooperate is to improve their own lot. An effective organizer of cooperative effort understands that the way to encourage participation by the group is to show them that by joining together, they are maximizing their own well-being. A true win-win situation.

If we make this cooperative effort and solve some of these devastating problems, we will have created a greater and more just society, and we will indeed benefit tremendously. Besides the enormous sense of pride and accomplishment that will result from solving these matters, we will be eliminating many of the threats that face our country, our children and the planet.

Chapter 6

Written in December 2008

Selected Excerpts from *Contagion: The Financial Epidemic That Is Sweeping the Global Economy*

Following are selected excerpts from "Contagion: The Financial Epidemic That Is Sweeping the Global Economy", a book Talbott wrote and published in December 2008. The publisher was John Wiley & Sons, Inc.

The United States Enters a Long Recession

Even the most stubborn real estate agent admits readily today that there is a housing price decline. Most agents, though, keep telling their clients that the worst is behind us and that prices are bottoming. For reasons described in an earlier chapter, this is not the case. I think that as of the end of 2008 the housing price decline is about half completed and that now housing price declines will move from subprime mortgages to prime mortgages in wealthier neighborhoods where most of the dramatic price appreciation during the real estate boom occurred.

This housing price decline is different from all others, not only because it is national, but because it started without a recession and significant job losses up front. Typically, it is a weak economy and a recession that causes job losses to be so significant as to force people to either default on their mortgages or sell their homes at lower prices and move to more moderate shelter. Here, because the housing boom was caused by loose lending with aggressive bank terms, the price decline was possible without a recession and without significant job losses, at least to start.

I will discuss the possibility that the housing price decline and the mortgage and banking crisis that ensued will cause a severe recession in the United States. I will then talk about how these housing problems, mortgage problems and the recessionary environment might spread internationally.

Even today, there are still some experts out there who are not forecasting a recession for the United States. Their reasoning is simple. These experts believe that the housing and financial problems to date are an asset problem and will have little impact on the real economy of jobs and economic activity in the country. When these experts calculate how an asset class and its decline in price can impact the general economy they typically refer to what is known as the wealth effect. They make comparisons between what happens when a stock market declines and people's wealth declines as a result, and what that means for their spending going forward and its impact on the general economy and GDP. The wealth effect is nothing more than calculating how much slower GDP will grow each year as a result of a shock or a decline in the wealth of American citizens.

Similarly, housing experts talk about the wealth effect when applied to housing price declines. Today, through the end of 2008, there has been a decline in the total aggregate market value of all residential real estate in the United States from $24 trillion to approximately $19 to $20 trillion. If the American people feel they are $4 to $5 trillion poorer, how will that impact their spending and consumption?

Advocates of the theory that housing-price declines have little to do with real economic output suggest that these declines have little impact on economic activity. They argue that the $5 trillion is not real because few people sell their house each year. It is a paper loss. Also, it is not $5 trillion that people invested in their homes from hard-earned equity, but rather it is simply giving back $5 trillion of profit that appreciated in the homes during the boom years. As a matter of fact, these profits were earned just since 2004 in the U.S. housing market.

So there is an argument from many supposed experts that the housing price decline will have little impact on the general economy. Even if you point out to these experts that the banks will suffer losses in the trillions, they reply that there are no real losers in this disruption because for every loss to a bank there is someone who gains, when someone defaults on a mortgage by definition, they keep the monies and the boats and cars and vacations that it bought.

As you might have guessed by now, I am not of this school of thought. I believe the housing price decline will have a significant impact on the economy, its growth and the stock market. Although I believe the wealth effect is real, especially for housing because of the great deal of leverage homeowners utilize and the breadth of ownership of houses relative to stocks, I don't see it as the key driver that transforms housing price losses into real economic output declines such as a decline in GDP.

I do believe that the value of residential housing in the United States at $24 trillion is such a large number that the country cannot experience 20 percent declines to date through the end of 2008, or expected 30 to 40 percent declines nationally without having far-reaching impacts on the $14 trillion economy.

The first impact on the economy is a direct impact. Industries closely related to housing will suffer. And these industries are going to suffer for a long time. The home-building industry is already in a severe depression. Home builders building new houses will suffer even more than typical homeowners living in existing homes because new homes act as sort of a buffer of new supply to the market when there is great demand for housing. But similarly, when that demand disappears and there is an increase in the existing home supply for sale by current owners, there is no need for new construction and new home building. It is one of those cyclical industries that go from enormous demand to zero overnight. Demand for new homes doesn't go down 2 percent in a bad year but trades off 60 percent to 70 percent. Existing homes for sale make up more than enough of the supply for all the homeownership demand.

There is a story that a small town just east of San Francisco by two hours and south of Sacramento by one hour saw its new homes that had sold for $720,000 a month earlier auctioned off for $320,000 after the crash. Of course, construction companies and developers that focused on condo development downtown in many major cities like Miami, San Diego, and Las Vegas also took a beating. They were building condominiums as fast as they could because the market, with the banks lending to them, were willing to pay two to three to four times the cost of construction for a new condominium. When prices collapsed, so did the condominium projects, many of them in a half-completed stage of construction.

In addition to home builders and condo developers, the next obvious direct impact on economic health and GDP is that hundreds of thousands of real estate brokers will see their livelihood greatly impaired.

Just as this housing crash begins to abate in five years or so, the bulk of the baby boom will be retiring and many elderly Americans will have moved onto nursing homes. The retirement of the baby boom will have a dramatic detrimental effect on GDP. But few people realize that as elderly people move out of their homes and into nursing and assisted-living facilities this dramatically increases the number of existing homes available for purchase. As Congress cracks down on illegal immigration and the elderly move out of their existing homes and into nursing homes over the next 20 years, America will have very little new home construction for the sustainable future.

So negative wealth effects will translate lower home prices into a weaker American economy and lower home prices will mean less activity in the real estate sector, broadly defined, which will mean lower growth rates in GDP. But I believe that the biggest impact from the housing crisis on the real economy is rarely discussed in the media or in academia. I believe that the biggest impact on the real economy will be due to the bank losses caused by the housing crisis from the sharp decline in mortgage asset values. The reason is that I believe that bank losses are the real key to understanding recessions.

Many people believe that recessions are normal cycles in business activity because they have always occurred. People look beyond trying to find a cause or a solution and rather accept them as inevitable and part of normal business activity. Let me try to explain why I think bank losses are the key to understanding recessions.

If the commercial banks ended up losing $1 trillion as a result of declining housing and mortgage prices, that is a direct contraction of their book equity. Because they are leveraged over 15 to 1, that means that unless they find a replacement for the lost equity through new equity issuance they may have to reduce their balance sheet and lend $15 trillion less. This is the deleveraging you hear about that is happening on Wall Street now. They have to get smaller or else they will not survive. So they won't be making any new loans to grow and they won't be renewing many of their favored clients' revolving credit facilities. They are going to be calling in many loans. This has to be negative on the economy.

But even small community banks are not off the hook. Although smaller regional banks were quick to sell residential mortgages upstream to mortgage packagers like Fannie Mae, they often involved themselves in substantial loans to local real estate developers and builders. Construction loans are a big part of a small regional bank's business and to the extent that a great deal of residential and commercial construction has now ceased, some of it with half-built buildings in the ground, these regional banks will face very substantial losses. These regional banks also have significant exposure to mall developers that are suffering as retailers begin to go bankrupt and will suffer substantial loan losses as the economy softens and the general business climate deteriorates.

The sheer magnitude of the size of the potential losses means that it will take years for the banks to deleverage and to replace their threatened equity capital base. No economy can effectively grow without a healthy banking climate as banks provide the necessary capital for new business formation, new building growth, new home growth and new factories and other business development.

Another argument made by the naysayers and those still in denial as to whether there will be a recession is that everything is temporary, that these are not permanent losses but only cyclical losses. Nothing could be further from the truth. These losses from the bank's perspective are indeed permanent. These mortgages are not going to spring back to full value. Housing prices that have declined are not going to re-inflate. The reason is that the bubble is bursting and is deflating a boom and returning to more normal pricing. The banks in the future are not going to lend 11 times your household income to buy a house. They might lend three to five times your income if you have a good job with demonstrable income, if you have a good credit score, if you are willing to put down a substantial down payment and if you have some verifiable means of demonstrating your job and income. This is a return to normalcy. Bank's losses are not going to be reversed. They are permanent. The effect on the general economy is permanent.

So the real question is not whether there is going to be an impact on the general economy and GDP from the housing price declines, but rather why hasn't it happened already and why hasn't it been more substantial? Why is GDP still growing through the middle of 2008? Housing prices are going to take five to seven years to reach bottom and so it is going to be a long, drawn-out process as this lower housing activity and the bank losses are reflected in the general economy.

So why hasn't the economy contracted quicker? The answer is that the average homeowner who either flipped houses or refinanced during the boom hasn't suffered a cash loss yet. Net, net, they've made money on the deal and have money in the bank. But, as people spend the last of their cash windfall they got from the refinancing of their overpriced home sales, and at the rate of consumption they are undertaking currently, it won't be long until these homeowners burn through these cash windfalls and the economy will suffer because there is no new bank lending to replace it.

Just because the economy does not go down today, does not mean it is not going to decline in the future. Finally, almost 2½ years into this housing price decline there are increases in the unemployment rate. Unemployment in the third quarter of 2008 was 6.1 percent and increasing. It is this unemployment that will lead to dramatic reductions in GDP growth. If your definition of a recession is two consecutive quarters of negative GDP growth, I can assure you that your definition will be satisfied, but it may be as late as early 2009. Once the recession kicks in, there is no guarantee that it will be short lived. As a matter of fact, I believe it will be a very long and very deep recession. I believe the tens of trillions of dollars that the banks will not lend in the future around the world will have a devastating impact on the global economy. And then the feedback cycles begin. As people are laid off in the construction and real estate industries, they end up consuming less and people begin to get laid off in other supporting industries. Automobiles, already in trouble, head south. People delay taking vacations. People delay buying cars. People stop buying boats. Retailers suffer, restaurants suffer, layoffs continue. As layoffs accelerate, economic activity slows, generating further layoffs. Business investment slows as business inventories build. Businesses lay off more employees.

I don't believe it is clear to any economists what stops this vicious downward cycle. Keynesians used to believe the government could step in and spend monies to stop such a devastating feedback loop. But today's economists believe that consumers and businesses are more fully rational and understand that phony government spending must be paid for with increased taxes or inflating the currency and so are less likely to fall for a government stimulation plan.

Milton Friedman once told me that eventually, even in a depression, unemployment will get so bad and wages will be so low that eventually there will be new hiring as people find productive uses for the newly unemployed and low-wage labor pool. I'm not sure I believe that. Milton Friedman tried to argue that wages were inflexible during the Great Depression and this prevented a quick recovery. I don't see it. Most workers were not in unions at the time of the Great Depression. I am no expert on the history of the Great Depression, but even I remember pictures of people carrying signs saying I will work for food. That doesn't sound like labor inflexibility to many. Laws were passed that tried to support wages, but it is hard to imagine they were immediately effective.

I am much more pessimistic that Milton Friedman. I believe that capitalism is based on trust. And that when that trust is violated, and contracts are not certain to be honored, and loans are not certain to be repaid, and when businesses hide losses, and when banks cannot be trusted with deposits, there is a real risk that all economic activity will stop. People will take their money out of banks and put it in their mattress. People will stop buying new things. Companies will cut production and workers. Companies will cut investment. It is not at all obvious to me how a country gets out of such a negative spiral. This is the risk that occurs. The biggest businesses and the largest banks and investment banks were allowed to run crazy for decades with little to no government regulation. The price must now be paid. I can only hope that the price is not too severe and that the country can pull out of these difficulties. But I also hope that the lesson is learned.

A Warning Shot Across the Bow

A problem of this magnitude could not have occurred unless there was something fundamentally wrong with the way the country is organized as a society. Simply blaming Wall Street or Washington D.C. for the problem won't cut it. It assumes complete ignorance on the part of average citizens. If Americans are indeed ignorant of the greatest problems facing the economy and the government, then that is a major problem for which Americans all bear responsibly. And if the people are not ignorant of these problems and do nothing to resolve them, that also is a problem that finger pointing cannot resolve.

Many far from Wall Street and Washington have been living far beyond their means on borrowed funds. Americans legally and morally committed to mortgage contracts with no intention of repaying them if things went bad. When the government acted unethically, citizens looked the other way. When told that congressmen were taking bribes from corporations they never got involved. When they heard the government was torturing prisoners they never got up out of their recliners and protested. When told that inequality in the country was exploding and that opportunity was disappearing for the middle class they never reacted. They didn't respond when the scientific community warned them they were harming the planet. They ran up government debts and unfunded Social Security and Medicare liabilities with no regard for how their children would repay them.

Newscaster and author Tom Brokaw described an earlier generation of Americans as "The Greatest Generation," many of whom were the sons and daughters of immigrants. They had next to nothing when they were growing up and this situation was only aggravated by the Great Depression. What made them great was a genuine concern for each other that extended far beyond simple self-interest.

In what must be the ultimate example of going from the frying pan to the fire, this generation's young people left the Depression behind only to find themselves fighting in the war. Plans for college were deferred in order to enlist. This was no regional conflict or police action. The entire world was at war. More than 50 million military and civilian casualties. More than 400,000 American military dead, but that pales in comparison to the estimated 20 million Soviets, 10 million Chinese, 6 million Poles, 5 million Germans and 2 million Japanese military personnel and civilians who perished in that war.

Enter the baby boom generation. Although not enormously spoiled with material things while growing up, they did have relatively stable home lives. Many boomers experienced rather self-absorbed childhoods involving binge drinking, experimenting with drugs and yes, listening to rock-and-roll. And yet the 1960s were this generation's brightest light as it was an attempt by the nation's youth to show concern for others. Young people organized and fought hard for the rights of women, minorities, the environment and to stop the killing of the Vietnam War.

At the time, many people thought that the torch had been passed to a new generation as John F. Kennedy suggested. Although the greatest generation was extremely hard working and tough, here was a new generation that was born after the Depression and World War II and so it was assumed would have a natural optimism about them. Many of this new generation attended at least some college, gaining some enlightenment about other cultures, human rights and human dignity. It was a heady optimistic time.

Most baby boomers are now in their fifties and are at the peak of their lifetime earnings capacity. And what have they seen fit to do with their new-found wealth and status? They have bought bigger and bigger homes, have invested in second vacation homes, have multiple cars and SUVs at their disposal and spend huge sums on fashion, restaurants, vacations and other self-indulgences. Rather than contributing more, so that others might suffer less, they have pushed through the largest tax cut in history, more than $4 trillion, the great majority of which goes to the richest Americans. They have run up government deficits, which when you exclude the illusionary Social Security surplus, exceed $500 billion annually and could quickly in the coming recession top $1 trillion annually.

This generation of Americans has shown little to no concern for other people around the world. Total foreign aid as a percentage of the U.S. GDP is less than 0.1 percent as billions suffer in poverty. AIDS is at an epidemic stage in Africa with some countries there reporting infection rates as high as 30 percent of their total adult population and more than 25 million dead already. Although China is indeed growing, it is the free market's infatuation with $1 a day labor that is its driving force. There has been no effort on behalf of the American consumer to reduce purchases of Chinese goods in order to properly address concerns there such as religion persecution, the illegality of union organizing, human rights violations, consumer rights and environmental issues.

This generation has sat idly by while the American government has pursued a foreign policy that ignores the pleas of the developing world to lift subsidies to American farmers, invades foreign countries without allies' support and tortures its captives.

This generation of American consumers is using more energy and creating more waste per person than any country in history. Oil prices are up considerably. World oil production is forecasted to peak and then decline in the near future and this generation continues to drive gas-guzzling SUVs and generously air condition their enormous homes. There is no effort to conserve energy or to actively develop alternative sources of energy like wind or solar power. In the most contemptuous act, Americans subsidized ethanol production, a means of stuffing food needed for the world's hungry into their gas tanks in order to take them to the mall.

Many people of this generation are retiring early to take advantage of generous pension plans and grab as many Social Security benefits as they can before the system collapses. They continue to vote to increase payroll taxes on the nation's youth, crippling the future economy just to continue to pay retirement benefits to themselves that no other future generation will ever see.

There is little chance that global warming will accelerate such that the baby boomer generation has to worry about it in its lifetime. It is a problem for future generations. Baby boomers don't have to worry about the education system declining; their kids go to private schools or have already graduated high school. There is no chance that the boomers will wake up tomorrow in poverty, and thanks to the repeal of inheritance taxes, there is no likelihood that their children or grandchildren will either. Hopefully, it is a small probability that a boomer would find himself in prison, and if so, it would most likely be a minimum security facility for white collar criminals. If gasoline goes to $6 a gallon, good, maybe the boomer's commute time will be faster once the poor get off the highways.

And so most of these problems are being ignored by this generation because they realize it is unlikely that they will be directly affected. The self-centered nature of this generation prevents them from applying energy and time to issues that do not immediately benefit themselves. They end up under-investing in societal solutions to global problems that at first blush appear to benefit others and have solutions that will create a better functioning society that protects the rights of all.

Somewhat surprisingly, ethical concern for a fellow man is the missing ingredient preventing people in this country from solving their most pressing problems. If Americans can look to help others, society benefits, and surprisingly ends up helping everyone. In what may sound confusing, it is in their self-interest to begin to care about the welfare of others as only then will major societal problems affecting them directly be resolved.

Market and governmental power have been the weapons of choice to date in addressing threats to prosperity and well-being, but they by themselves are not enough. Economic markets are ill suited for solving many of the complex problems facing us that require more cooperation than competition and world governments have enormous shortcomings that prevent these issues from being properly addressed. In addition to business and government involvement, civil society must begin to take a more active and ethical role to ensure a proper productive balance of this truly holy triangle. Government corruption and corporate lobbying power may be the most visible problem, but wars, poverty, environmental degradation of the planet, human rights violations, education problems, energy self-sufficiency, world health and the commercialization of the media will not be addressed and cannot be solved without direct citizen involvement.

Ethical action is not limited to just finding a way to get politicians to stop lying and businesspeople to stop cheating. It also means that the people themselves must elevate ethical concerns in all their decision making. Simply speaking, acting ethically can be thought of as just doing the right thing and showing as much concern for others as we have shown to date for ourselves. Hopefully, there can be a discussion about proper ethical action even if Americans are not ethically perfect— or else I would have to stop right here.

First and foremost, it is the people who have to lead on this front by acting ethically and behaving morally before I can expect the world situation to improve. With no moral outrage on behalf of the people there can be no progress in addressing concerns on how businesses and government act. Unless people elevate their concern for others and the health of the group, these problems will continue to languish. And without firm ethical accountability of elected representatives and business leaders, suggested solutions will never translate into implementable programs.

Somewhat magically, if the people do find a new moral voice and begin to act in the public good, not only will general society improve, but problems directly threatening them and their families will quickly begin to disappear. Fears about their retirement plans, the proper education of their children, adequate health care for their family, their own self-worth and a general worry that the world is headed to hell in a hand-basket will all begin to subside. Most importantly, people will start feeling good about themselves again as they will realize they are not alone, but rather important and integral parts of a world community. Their work, their ideas and their lives will have meaning again. As opposed to worrying about home mortgage rates, the latest fashion craze, music video news and the latest political corruption scandal, people will start devoting their time to real problems the world faces knowing that solutions are achievable and real people, including themselves, will benefit.

The key to uncovering this true path to greater prosperity and societal well-being lies in marrying a knowledge of government, economics and ethics. One would not be surprised to learn that politicians and ethics are a bad mix, but there must be a way of transferring this new-found ethical action on behalf of a people through their government representatives and into practical governmental programs.

Economics and the free market have also made strange bedfellows with ethics over time as Adam Smith's free-trade theories are based on people acting narrowly in their self-interest and yet society still benefitting. This is not to suggest that acting in one's self-interest is inherently unethical. But, depending on circumstances, ignoring the public interest or the effects of your actions on others can indeed be unethical. Proved as an effective system for providing many traditional goods and services, free-market economics has little to offer in the study of problems for which self-interested action exacerbates rather than alleviates the situation.

It should disturb everyone that the fundamental premise on which all modern economic theory is based is that people are assumed to always act rationally — and rational action is partly defined as people acting solely in their self-interest. How could such a self-centered theory explain young soldiers selflessly volunteering to die for the love of their country, international aid workers risking their lives for little to no income to assist the sick and dying of the world, mothers sacrificing exciting business careers to spend more time at home with their children, people shortening their lives by smoking tobacco and drinking alcohol, the poor wasting their few precious dollars on lotteries with little chance of winning and teachers and professors accepting less pay than they might earn elsewhere simply because they just feel good about helping the next generation learn.

Global free markets are so pervasive and powerful in the world today that you would expect that if free markets acting alone could have solved these problems, the problems would have already been solved. In other words, it should not be surprising that many, if not all, of the major threats and problems that remain unsolved and continue to imperil an individual's well-being today are those that the traditional free market allocation of economic goods and services could not easily handle. In fact, they are. Almost universally, they share common characteristics that make them exceedingly difficult for the free market to address.

It as if billions of self-interested free-market profit-oriented entrepreneurial businesspeople have raced about the planet for centuries solving every problem and satisfying every consumer need they could, so long as they themselves also benefited. As a result many traditional goods and services allocation problems have indeed been solved. And thanks to the beauty of the properly regulated free market, most of this activity has happened almost automatically with little central planning or government interference. But these same free-market participants have put little energy into solving those problems that provide little direct benefit to themselves and yet are critical for the proper overall functioning society.

Originally, some geneticists and social Darwinists suggested that such concern for anyone other than one's own gene pool was counter to evolutionary theory and not sustainable in human behavior. They tried to argue that in a world of survival of the fittest, it was greed that was most important to survival. Many of these same socio-biologists are now beginning to recognize that there exists in man and his ancestors many examples of genetic-inspired behavior that encourages cooperation and that this very cooperation aids in survival of the group and thus of the individual's gene pool.

Even if there were no genetic basis for cooperative, unselfish behavior, humans exercising their free will and creative ingenuity would invent it if they deemed it helpful in better organizing and advancing their society and providing greater opportunities for themselves. No one is limited in thought and action by their genes.

It turns out the movie *Spiderman* had it right. "With great power comes great responsibility." The challenge of this definitional approach to moral action is that it puts a heavier burden on the truly talented than it does on the mundane, blissfully ignorant, poorly educated huddled masses. Although a brilliant successful person could claim enormous opportunity costs if she had to forego her personal career to aid society, this same person would be invaluable to organizing and solving many of the world's worst problems.

For solutions to be found to the world's most pressing problems, people are going to have to wage war on the establishment as it exists today. Through globalization, an elaborate system has been created, led by the United States, which is pushing completely free-market capitalism on the world as the solution to all of its problems. You do not have to be a conspiracy nut to realize that multinational corporations are the most powerful organizing force on the planet today and that their sole objective is the amoral pursuit of increased profits globally. The major benefit to these corporations going global has been their transcendence from any single government's regulation or taxation.

And so, the world today is dominated by a system that favors market solutions to most everything, sees the corporation as the prime vehicle for action, virtually controls many of the world's governments and emphasizes open markets and globalization as the cure-all to the world's problems.

Advanced capitalist countries, because they emphasize competition instead of cooperation, self-interest rather than public interest and consumption instead of altruism end up creating a mind set in their people that is distinctly different from the less capitalist, less developed countries. World travelers are always somewhat surprised at how warm and friendly the lesser developed countries of the world are as compared to the advanced countries. It is easy to assume that this lack of killer spirit is the reason that these countries have not developed faster, but the opposite may be true. It may be that all people of the world are cooperative and sharing and compassionate until they adopt capitalism and begin to industrialize. It may be the advanced countries' people who are different and abnormal, not the people in the developing world. It may be that the advanced world has a problem that has gone undiagnosed until now.

In traveling, the first thing you notice about Americans, the British and people from other advanced countries is that they are obsessed with status. They talk about their material possessions and work accomplishments in an attempt to demonstrate their more dominant position. Such status seekers are inherently insecure and their arrogance is but a defense mechanism. Such people begin to define themselves in terms of their incomes, their jobs and their material possessions. No wonder they are insecure. If a person's identity is defined by such temporal and material objects then it makes sense that the person will be insecure as to whom he or she really is.

Second, many people from advanced countries come across as extremely self-centered and greedy when viewed through the eyes of someone who lives in the developing world. The hoarding, gross consumption and wastefulness of many in the advanced world is disturbing to people in the developing world.

The solution to the major problems facing the United States today is a societal-wide reemphasis on cooperation, compassion and concern for others. The first step is to better understand how Americans became this greediest of generations to see if there is not an as yet undisclosed path out of the darkness of such self-centered behavior. Unless people's concern for their neighbors can be re-stimulated, there will never be the true moral outrage by the majority of the population that is required for real cooperative action necessary to address these threats to society.

Specialization of labor, the hierarchical structure of corporations, greater communication abilities, rapid technological obsolescence and globalization have all led to greater insecurity on behalf of the individual. Increased insecurity in a fast-moving world is the prime culprit to explain why this generation turned so inward in its greed and self-interest. Until people feel comfortable with their own well-being and identity it is difficult to show concern for others. Greater personal security comes with increased confidence that you are leading a productive and good life, not in greater material possessions.

People who are not sure of their own identity turn to other ways of defining who they are. People often define themselves by the status of their job, what school they went to, what neighborhood they live in or what kind of car they drive.

Greater prosperity itself may ironically fuel more intense feelings of self-interest rather than satisfy individual needs and wants and thus be an enemy of cooperative effort for the societal good. Experts are studying whether absolute wealth or relative wealth brings greater pleasure to humans. If the answer is relative wealth, it might provide another possible reason why this baby boom generation has gotten so wrapped up in itself. Clearly, this generation has lived a rather charmed life of luxury relative to any other generation and Americans have enjoyed a material wealth available to few others on the planet. But if relative wealth is the measure, there can be only one person with the nicest car, the biggest house, the best paying job; the rest of us have to suffer in relative despair.

In the book *The Progress Paradox*, Gregg Easterbrook presents startling statistics that the American baby boom generation has a level of wealth, health and prosperity that others could only imagine. The average life expectancy in America has grown from 41 years to 71 years since 1900. Polio, smallpox, measles and rickets are all virtually eliminated. Starvation has been eliminated, although hunger still plagues the poorest citizens. Leisure time has expanded. Educational opportunities have exploded. A much greater percentage own their own homes today, most with central air and heating and many with swimming pools.

Surprisingly, Easterbrook also reports that this generation of Americans is much less happy than earlier generations. Surveys structured to measure happiness show a broad trend that people are significantly less happy today than people of 40 years ago. Reported cases of depression are up tenfold in 40 years, a statistic that is probably biased upward by better diagnostic techniques today.

Easterbrook has done a great service in demonstrating that greater material wealth and incomes do not automatically translate into greater happiness. He even provides a per capita inflection point of $10,000, below which greater personal incomes in countries around the world seem to provide greater happiness and above which happiness seems to decline with greater income. Below $10,000 of income, any increased earnings go to providing real necessities such as food, clothing, shelter, education and medical care and thus alleviate real suffering and allow for the provision of basic human rights. Above

$10,000, something strange happens. People earn more, have more disposable income, more leisure time, bigger homes, more cars and boats, longer and more luxurious vacations and yet, the more they make and spend the less happy they are.

Easterbrook is joined by George Will, Milton Friedman and other conservative scholars who make a fundamental error in trying to explain this apparent dichotomy that greater material welfare does not necessarily bring greater happiness. In their heart they believe that greater incomes and material wealth should make people happier because that is the basis for supposedly rational economics. Namely, that market participants are not only self-interested, but that they will always value more of good things. Two houses are better than one, three ski boats are better than two and four-wheel drive is better than two. The belief that more is better is so endemic to their theory of economics and human behavior that it leads them to the following mistaken conclusion with regard to the dichotomy.

They reason, "If humans are much better off materially and are less happy it must be because humans just don't know how good they have it." These same people who insist that humans are rational and informed enough to make complex pricing, purchasing and investing decisions in the economic marketplace suddenly turn out to be so dumb as to not even be able to judge how well off they are. The public is the best judge of what is good for them and what might improve their welfare, and it is this fundamental premise that is the basis of democratic government.

What is wonderful is that Americans, as well the other advanced countries of the world, have incomes that satisfy basic survival and human rights needs and so are perfectly positioned to adopt a more societal-friendly posture to helping solve the really big problems the planet faces. And it turns out it doesn't look like you will be losing any happiness by turning your attention outward; as a matter of fact, you may help others experience greater happiness and in turn find your own lives more fulfilled, more meaningful, oh, and yes, perhaps more happy.

Obviously, not all members of the American baby boom contributed to being the world's greediest. There are some who have not bought into this age of rampant consumerism and not joined the me generation. The same people who tried to end the war in the 1960s were the ones who fought to clean up the environment in the 1970s, marched for women's rights in the 1980s, demonstrated in support of animal rights in the 1990s and are forming nongovernmental organizations (NGOs) today to address the abuses of globalization.

This generation had it all — prosperity, education, security, family, friends and global access to information and markets — but they failed to deliver. The most important problems facing the earth were not addressed, not because they were not fully understood, but because this generation didn't have the time as they were too busy clothing their children in designer outfits, furnishing their second homes and seeing that their pools got cleaned.

The problems in Washington and on Wall Street, and for that matter, in Africa as well as rural poor America, begin with us. The housing boom and bust was a symptom of a broken regulatory system that was allowed to fester because of the corruption of corporate lobbying and campaign bribes to elected representatives. But it is not the only problem that society needs to address. Corporate lobbyists have prevented health-care reform, energy reform, global warming initiatives, minimum wage legislation, social security reform and peaceful resolution of conflicts around the world.

After people in this country clean up Washington, throw the lobbyists out and properly regulate Wall Street, hopefully there will be time for some self-reflection. Have Americans become consumed by status seeking? Are they truly any happier with their enormous consumption and debts? Is there something to life beyond satisfying self-interest? If this crisis was a shot across the bow, maybe it will be the clarion call needed to make people rethink how they wish to live their lives, to decide what is truly important in life and what ultimately they hope to accomplish with their short time here on the planet.

Chapter 7

Written in January 2009

"Obama Must Let the Economy Shrink"

Originally published in the San Francisco Chronicle on January 6, 2009.

Barack Obama, as we speak, is putting together his big economic plan to be unveiled after his inauguration. While including some tax cuts for average Americans, it appears the main emphasis of his plan is a $1 trillion-plus-multiyear-government stimulus of the U.S. economy. Interest rates are already at .25 percent and cannot be effectively lowered much more. Bank lending, even between banks, has pretty much ceased. The stock prices of most financial institutions are off more than 75 percent. It certainly looks as if something has to be done.

But what? America is hamstrung. We already had approximately $10 trillion of debt going into this crisis, and now it looks like President Bush and Treasury Secretary Henry Paulson have spent or made guarantees of an additional $8 trillion, and that doesn't include the $5 trillion of questionable Fannie Mae and Freddie Mac assets the government already has absorbed. Even the federal government's ability to borrow has a limit. Because Americans do not save, there will come a day when foreign governments and foreign institutions simply will say, "No more; we have had our fill of U.S. Treasury debt." With a rapidly shrinking $14 trillion economy, the United States' day when its credit card is refused may not be far off.

I don't blame President-elect Obama for his stimulus plan in this economic environment. I don't even blame his economic advisers. It is the entire field of economics that is wanting.

For too long, economists have fallen in love with their mathematical models of certainty and have ignored how poorly these models reflect the real world. Both Bush's economic advisers, who wanted to emphasize trickle-down tax cuts to America's biggest corporations and our wealthiest citizens, and Obama's economic advisers, who wish to cut taxes on working Americans and increase government spending tremendously to revitalize the economy, have it wrong. The problem we have is too much debt-financed consumption. And yet the proposed solution by both parties is to finance more consumption with additional debt.

Economic growth in America, and for much of the world, during the last 10 years has been somewhat illusionary. Increased consumption by individuals, corporations and the government that funded this economic expansion in the United States was financed with an increase of total debt, from $25 trillion, 10 years ago to $60 trillion today. They have all spent beyond their means and used debt to purchase things they could not afford. This is not sustainable.

Individuals, banks and corporations now have to repay their debts and begin to save, so they will not have the money to make additional purchases of goods and services.

This means the real gross domestic product of the United States is going to shrink. It has to return to the more sustainable level we saw before all this borrowing. Just as home prices must return to their more reasonable level before the introduction of loose lending and crazy mortgage instruments, so the GDP of the United States has to decline to a level that balances shopping with savings by it citizenry.

Instead, our leaders are launching tax cuts, fiscal stimulus plans and taxpayer bailouts, all of which increase government debt that must be repaid by our children. There is nothing wrong with allowing GDP to return to its levels of eight years ago, other than that corporations today have too much debt to remain solvent under those conditions.

The way out of this difficult time is through inflation of our currency - the government needs to print more money. Inflation, which no one likes and which can be very damaging to an economy, is the only way to deflate the value of debts on everyone's balance sheets at the same time.

The second step is to develop a very rapid personal and corporate bankruptcy process. There is no reason restructuring and bankruptcy should take years.

Obama is a self-described incrementalist, but in a world that is on the brink of financial collapse, we cannot afford incremental steps. Incrementalism may be the right approach to solving long-term problems such as global climate change. Unfortunately, there is no guarantee our financial system will survive months, much less years. We have very little room for error.

We must make the right decisions, and we must make them quickly.

Chapter 8

Written in April 2009

Selected Excerpts from *The 86 Biggest Lies on Wall Street*

Following are selected excerpts from "The 86 Biggest Lies on Wall Street", a book Talbott wrote and published in April 2009. The publisher was Seven Stories Press.

Lie #6 - This was a random event, like a hundred-year flood, that occurs naturally in the markets every fifty to one hundred years and could not be avoided.

Alan Greenspan tried to argue that this financial crisis was completely unexpected, impossible to have been predicted — a hundred-year flood, a purely random event. While Alan Greenspan was officially a government representative, he really spoke for the entire free market community that believed that markets should not be regulated. He was a major advocate and follower of Ayn Rand's philosophy that argued that regulation only got in the way of the individual spirit of human enterprise, best exemplified in a completely free market. Remember, Ayn Rand was a novelist, and novels are fiction (Acemoglu).

First of all, I am living proof that this crisis was predictable since I predicted it in my housing books of 2003 and 2006. You can argue, as one reader tried to on Amazon.com, that I was just lucky in my predictions. But given their exacting accuracy, that would have to make me the luckiest man on the earth. I not only warned that housing prices would decline, I said their biggest declines would be in Florida and California and that the country would see 25 percent price declines while individual cities on the coast would see declines north of 55 percent. I explained that the mortgage market would enter a crisis, and that because the majority of banks' assets were held in real estate-related fields, the banks themselves would be threatened with insolvency. I predicted the complete demise of the private mortgage insurance market, which has now occurred. I suggested that Fannie Mae and Freddie Mac would never make it through the crisis. In my first housing book I suggested the problem would be national, which violated the age-old promise that all real estate is local, and in my second book I suggested the problem would be international, which has now proven true. Ironically, the reviewer on Amazon.com who originally called me lucky about my predictions logged back on after Fannie and Freddie went bankrupt and conceded that I had been right about them — but maintained that I was just continuing with my lucky streak.

No, this was not a random event. This was not due to the general business cycle. It had a real cause, and that cause was fundamental and structural. Our government, our financial markets, our largest financial institutions and our biggest corporations entered into a corrupt business enterprise to rip off the American consumer and taxpayer. The entire mortgage financing business and much of Wall Street itself was corrupted and through their campaign donations and lobbying they were able to corrupt our government.

Real estate agents pushed people into ever larger homes they could not afford, appraisers provided appraisals that were disconnected from reality in order to make fees and mortgage brokers falsely changed and fraudulently manipulated mortgage applications to ensure that deals got done. Commercial banks packaged junk securities and called them AAA with the paid assistance of the rating agencies who were part of the complete criminal conspiracy. The purchaser of the securities, the world's largest pension funds, government institutions, international banks and sovereign debt funds may not have been corrupt, but they were certainly ignorant. They relied on a AAA rating knowing full well that the rating agency was being paid by the issuer, not the investor and did little further credit analysis before investing.

This entire fraudulent scheme could never have occurred without the complicity of our government representatives. But they did not sell themselves cheaply. The largest contributors to the campaigns of our congressmen and presidents over the last fifteen years have been the National Association of Realtors, the Mortgage Bankers Association, the American Bankers Association (representing commercial banks), hedge funds, investment banks on Wall Street and of course Fannie Mae and Freddie Mac. Our Congress was paid to stand down. They were paid not to enforce existing regulations, not to pass any new legislation and to deregulate, to remove old regulation from the books to allow our financial institutions the ability to do whatever they wished. Financial institutions and their executives took out hundreds of billions of dollars in profits and management bonuses during the housing and mortgage boom, so they were willing to risk some losses to keep the game going.

No, this was not a random event. This was a pre-planned and direct attack on the American consumer and the American taxpayer. Americans are now losing their jobs, losing their homes and putting their families under tremendous stress because of the actions of Wall Street, our largest financial institutions and our biggest corporations. The fact that they paid off our government representatives for their complicity should not shift the blame to government. This was free enterprise at its best.

Lie #10 - Capitalism works equally well in all industries.

Capitalism's supporters would like it to be the case that capitalism is equally effective in all industries since it encourages individuals and corporations to maximize profits and thereby the well-being of society.

Ironically, now that the financial markets have collapsed, it might be performing a disservice to suggest that all of capitalism is broken. Critics of capitalism have utilized the recent financial crisis to suggest that all of capitalism is a failure and that major changes must be made to all industries or that capitalism itself might have to die.

If we can show, however, that the financial markets and Wall Street are unique in some way, different from other industries and that Wall Street is an example of how purely unregulated capitalism does not work well in the banking system, then we may be able to save other industries from abandoning a successful capitalist approach.

The banking system is unique in one regard. It deals with very long-lived assets and liabilities. These assets, like homes and businesses, can survive a hundred years and their mortgages can certainly last thirty and forty years. This is far beyond the life expectancy of many senior managements at these banking institutions and it certainly extends beyond their working years.

This means that managements at these institutions can do some fairly stupid things that will impact profits negatively over a long-term horizon, but that might generate additional cash flow in the short term. For example, a bank executive could push his institution into highly profitable subprime mortgages knowing full well that the defaults on such mortgages will not occur for years in the future, long after he is gone.

Capitalism, of course, does not guarantee that there will not be individual instances of bad management in the market. But the concept of free-market capitalism is that such bad players will be punished by the marketplace and that their firms will not profit.

The problem with long-lived asset industries like banking is that the punishment is too long in coming (William J. Talbott). Consider this example: You own a donut shop in the middle of town and a new competitor opens up across the street, selling donuts for what everyone knows is half the cost of actually making them. The bad news is they will get 100 percent of the customers in town; the good news is they will very quickly go bankrupt since selling products below cost is not a very profitable long-run enterprise strategy. Your short-term profits might suffer, but you will not feel pressure to match their silly pricing as you know they will very quickly succumb to the pressures of the market and go bankrupt.

Now, suppose you run a mortgage bank in town and a newcomer opens a mortgage bank across the street offering no money down on very low interest, negative amortization, forty-year mortgage loans. Again, the bad news is that you will lose market share and customers. The further bad news is this new mortgage banker will not immediately go out of business. It will be years and maybe decades before his mispricing of risk shows up in actual defaults and foreclosures and ends up bankrupting his business. In the meantime, he will either garner 100 percent market share or you will be forced to match his pricing. This is what happened with the mortgage crisis in America. Because of the long-lived nature of the banking business, some aggressive and unscrupulous bankers began to misprice risk and offer terms that in the long-run were not profitable, but in the short run turned out to be enormously so. The sad fact is that well-meaning and well-managed banking operations had to match their stupid pricing terms or face extinction themselves.

Banking is not the only long-lived asset and liability business in the world for which capitalism does not work perfectly well. The insurance business has long been recognized as a very long-lived liability industry in which companies taking in positive cash flow in premiums have to maintain sufficient capital in the long run to honor their insurance contracts and that is why the insurance industry is so highly regulated. There is no way short of regulation that the marketplace can prevent an unscrupulous competitor from dominating the insurance business by offering lower premiums with no intention of ever making contractually obligated insurance payoffs.

It is the reason why all long-lived asset and liability industries must be regulated.

And this is the key. If the banking industry or the donut industry were a simple stand-alone segment of our entire GDP, it would be one thing. But the truth is that the banking system is the fundamental credit system for all of our industries. We are in a difficult position where the key component to our entire financial and economic health is our banking system and yet we are now realizing that it must be regulated since it does not perform well under completely unregulated capitalist terms.

The solution is self-apparent. Many shorter-lived asset and liability industries like donut shops can be allowed to continue fairly unregulated, letting competition to do its level best to maximize profitability for the industry as a whole. But banking and other long-lived asset liability industries must be regulated and if we do not regulate them, we will force our economy, including all other industries, into violent boom and bust recessions and depressions as the banking industry itself tries to deal and cope with the unregulated nature of its existence. The choice is simple. Deregulate banks and force the world to suffer. Properly regulate banks with regard to their leverage and the riskiness of the businesses they enter and you will eliminate the driving cause of most recessions and depressions.

Lie #23- The stock market will bounce back soon to pre-crisis levels and so will the economy.

If you turn on any of the financial news television programs on cable television, you will hear a constant litany of folks trying to predict the bottom of this market. Once the bottom is reached, it is assumed that the market will bounce back to where it had been trading before the financial crisis.

As a matter of fact, if you look back at the historic recessions in the United States this is pretty much the case. Recessions last from months to years but the stock market eventually bounces back to the pre-recession levels. Thus, successful investing only requires the difficult task of identifying the true bottom, because once you know you have invested at the bottom you will benefit from the bounce back to "more normal times."

But this recession is different from all others. Like the Great Depression, it was preceded by a very significant bubble in residential real estate as well as many other asset classes in the world. Housing prices, which started this whole mess, may at some point stop going down, but they are not going to bounce back up to their previous level. Banks are not going to start lending again at ten times people's combined incomes, but rather will demand serious down payments, valid credit reports, income verification and more modest total lending amounts of five to five and a half times a couple's income. If banks lend 50 percent less than they used to for buying homes, then homes have to come down further in price — unless home buyers are willing to put up substantially larger down payments, which I doubt.

The mortgage market, the student loan market, the credit card market and the auto loan market all depended on creating securitized pass-through vehicles like CDOs that could achieve AAA ratings and fool long-term investors into making bad investments. That game is also over. I do not see how anyone will accept a rating agency's AAA rating as a reason to invest in a complex security going forward.

The banks and the financial industry generated tremendous returns for their stockholders by increasing debt leverage from twelve to twenty-five times their equity base. Now they must deleverage. They will not be able to generate the same returns on equity given the lower leverage.

China and the emerging markets were dependent on debt financed consumption in the United States and Europe to fund their growth, which now must slow considerably. Even pharmaceutical and health care companies, which should benefit from the aging of the population in the United States, are going to see limits placed on them in terms of the amount of money Americans can spend on health care.

There is no reason to believe that this stock market will bounce back to its pre-crisis levels. Pre-crisis, price earnings multiples were high and companies' gross margins were at all-time records. This recession will be long and painful, with real GDP declines and growth prospects of individual companies going forward will have to be curtailed.

Therefore, it is much more likely that this post-crisis environment will not be a V-shaped rebound, but more of an L. We will head down to a more normal level of spending and stay there. Remember, pre-crisis, much of the GDP growth that was accomplished was due to individuals', companies' and the government's massive consumption based on increased borrowing. Now not only has new borrowing ceased, but the excessive borrowing of the pre-crisis period must be repaid. Removing this debt financed consumption from GDP and assuming a more modest growth in government expenditures means that GDP may be overstated by as much as 20 to 25 percent. It will take years for the post-crisis world to adjust to lower levels of consumption and lower GDP and stock prices will reflect that by remaining depressed for years.

The final nail in the coffin is that, demographically speaking, the baby boom is on the verge of retiring and leaving the productive workforce. Not only will we lose their productive efforts, but they will continue to age, requiring much greater state assistance with their retirement and health care. This cannot be good for the economy.

The Real Reform Needed on Wall Street

Now that you have read through the biggest lies on Wall Street, you can see that there are many fundamental changes that must occur before our capital markets and our economy get straightened out. There is much lying and cheating going on in the system, both on Wall Street and in Washington, but very little progress will be made until the root causes of this crisis are uncovered and corrected. Today, much of what has been tried to fix the economy has failed. I haven't liked any of the approaches taken to date at all.

Hank Paulson and George Bush originally said that they were going to be buying underwater mortgage securities from financial institutions as a way of freeing up capital for the banks. This made no sense to me because I did not see this as a liquidity crisis, but as a bank solvency crisis. Buying mortgages at discount prices from the banks would do nothing more than create additional losses for the banks, which would further threaten their solvency.

After Paulson woke up to that fact, he ended up not utilizing any of the TARP funds to buy underwater mortgages as he had promised Congress. Instead he turned around and gave $350 billion to some of his closest friends on Wall Street in the financial industry. In addition to these direct equity contributions and bailouts, he guaranteed $300 billion of Citigroup's assets. And all of this without asking debt investors in these companies to take a single dollar of losses.

Obama's announced stimulus plans also leave something to be desired. His combination of tax cuts and government spending means that the government will be spending an additional $800 billion. This means that the government deficit may approach $2.0 trillion in 2009.

A very simple explanation of what got us into this mess is that our citizens, our businesses, our banks and our government utilized a very low interest rate environment to dramatically increase borrowing and increase consumption. Now, both Bush and Obama plan on getting us out of this crisis by increasing debt to stimulate further consumption while holding interest rates near zero. This has to be the first time that the medicine given for an ailment is another heavy dose of exposure to whatever caused the illness in the first place. We can call the plan the hair of the dog; it reminds me of a drunk who has a drink first thing in the morning to try to cure his hangover.

I think policy makers are rehashing the same playbook that they all read in graduate school: C + I + G = GDP. They think that as C, consumption, goes down, GDP can be maintained by increasing G, government spending or I, private investment. While their arithmetic is correct, I don't think it reflects the real world well at all.

If government spending could replace consumption in an economy, then all countries would do this. They would just have their governments increase spending whenever their GDP faltered. I can't think of a case where this has ever worked. FDR is credited by some for spending enormous amounts of money that helped us get out of the Great Depression, but other economists believe his emphasis on government spending prolonged the depression. For years, it was common knowledge that what really ended the Great Depression was government spending on WWII, but even now this assumption is being attacked by new academic research. It never made sense to me that it was economically productive to build tanks and bombs and planes for war so that you can go and destroy productive capacity in the world.

And what nobody is addressing is that we are not paying for this increase in government spending or for any tax cuts offered. We are borrowing the money and our children will have to pay it back. It is as if we are saying that we do not want to live with one dollar less of GDP, a bit less consumption or a slightly different lifestyle from what we are used to and in order to maintain our lifestyle we are willing to tax our children so that they will have to have a lower standard of living. It makes no sense.

A country cannot continue to borrow from its future generations forever. Somebody has to be willing to lend to that country. Especially in America, where the savings rate until just recently has been negative. The only way Obama and Bush's plan of implementing additional borrowing to fund even more unnecessary consumption will work is if foreign governments and foreign institutions continue to lend to the United States. It is not clear to me that they are going to forever.

Even before any Obama stimulus plan or tax cut was taken into account, the Office of Management and Budge expected $1.2 trillion deficits in 2009. Layering on the Obama stimulus plan means that the deficit in 2009 could approach $2 trillion. Given that GDP is currently contracting from its high of $14 trillion, this means the operating deficit of our government may exceed 15 percent of our GDP. This will not only be the highest record level ever set, it will be the highest by a factor of two.

And, it doesn't count the biggest expenses of our government, namely Social Security and Medicare. It is estimated that unfunded liabilities for Medicare and Social Security will add another $35 trillion to the government's obligations, going forward on a present value basis.

If this recession continues for a number of years, one can easily see how the total government debt will quickly exceed $20 trillion and how the total liabilities of the government will exceed $50 trillion. Assuming that GDP shrinks into the $12 to $13 trillion range over the next few years, this means that our debt will be approaching four times our GDP.

This is an enormous number. It would put us in the category of the worst-capitalized, poorest developing countries of the world. Whether the United States has sufficient borrowing capacity to accomplish all of this government spending is no longer a hypothetical question. When our debt approaches these levels, foreign investors and foreign governments most certainly will pull back on their investments in America. China has recently announced that they are "worried" about their investments in US Treasury securities. If foreign countries and their largest institutions stop lending to America, the game is over. By running larger and larger annual operating deficits, we run the risk of not only increasing our debt to the point that foreigners revolt, but of creating an environment in which much of our government operations will have to shut down because the government will not have sufficient cash flow if its borrowing ability is taken away. We are running deficits and borrowing money to fund those deficits. This cannot go on for long.

I don't think we can borrow and spend our way out of this recession and I'm especially suspicious of government spending, which has never been that productive in the past. How can borrowing a dollar from me so the government can spend it be considered a stimulus to the economy? Much of the trillion dollars that Obama plans to spend is going to go to the states because they are running shortfalls. They won't hire any new people. They will just continue to pay themselves rather high salaries relative to the private sector. Another large chunk of the stimulus package will go to increasing and extending unemployment benefits. Again, an admirable cause, but it does nothing for creating new jobs.

Finally, the government is talking about creating new jobs to build highways, repair bridges, build wireless Internet access points in cities, invest in infrastructure, build electricity grids and so on. Such large construction projects will provide work for day laborers, but very few Americans today work in the manual labor sector. It isn't like 1930, when creating jobs digging ditches helped out most Americans. Today construction jobs will help very few Americans. It's very difficult for the government to figure out a stimulus plan that will employ doctors, lawyers, bankers and other professionals. That is why the private sector should create jobs, not government.

It would be much better than trying to artificially stimulate the economy to just allow the economy to contract. It had reached unsustainable levels because everybody was borrowing and consuming beyond their means. The economy needs to come back to a more reasonable level, just like house prices have to return to the reasonable level they were at before bank and mortgage lending went crazy.

If GDP were allowed to shrink back to 2002 levels, it wouldn't be the worst situation. Many of us were doing quite well in 2002. It doesn't mean that unemployment has to explode, but to the extent that productivity has improved, to achieve full employment we might each need to take a 5 to 10 percent haircut in our salaries. I think this would be an inexpensive way of getting us out of this crisis that otherwise threatens all of our jobs, our nation and the world.

But companies, especially highly leveraged companies, cannot survive if GDP contracts. Their debt loads will push them into bankruptcy. This massive amount of debt our corporations and financial institutions have taken on is going to have to be dealt with one way or the other. I recommend creating a new bankruptcy court process that last for weeks rather than years so that companies can very quickly reorganize in bankruptcy and come out with better operating plans, new managements and less debt.

Another recommendation is to allow the government to inflate the currency and purposely cause substantial inflation — possibly as much as 20 percent inflation over the next couple of years. It sounds like a crazy idea, given how devastating inflation can be to an economy. But this is not a properly functioning economy. If you introduce substantial short-term inflation, everybody — consumers, the government businesses and the banks — will all see the real value of their debts decrease. This is what the world needs right now. Debtors need to be forgiven for a portion of the debt that they have taken on. Inflating the currency across the board does this quickly and efficiently and is appropriate since nearly everybody is over-leveraged. Assets around the world have dropped some $30 trillion, but the corresponding debt has not budged.

Well into the second year of this recession, I cannot say that our government or the financial sector has developed an effective strategy for getting out. Throwing money at bankrupt firms in taxpayer bailouts before creditors took a single hit to their debt investments not only made no sense but was completely ineffective in slowing the weakening economy. Giving money outright to the largest financial institutions in the country may have staved off bankruptcy for those firms in the short run but, again, did too little to free up the credit markets or to increase lending to consumers and business.

President Obama's efforts to stimulate the economy by throwing money at Main Street through tax cuts to individuals and dramatic increases in government spending could easily fail. I don't think it will create enough jobs and I don't think it will slow the economy's decline.

So where are we then? In six months, in December 2009, we will be entering the third year of the most serious global recession the world has seen in its history. There is a very real risk that it could become a depression if we continue to make mistakes in how we address the problem. Here then, are the fundamental reforms I am recommending that must happen to stabilize our capital markets, to return confidence to our economy and to fix our broken institutions.

First: we need not just greater transparency, but complete transparency of all assets, liabilities, guarantees, credit default swap exposures and any other liabilities our corporations and our financial institutions are facing. I'm not talking about an extra two pages in an annual report. I'm talking about a disclosure that might extend to 1,000 pages and could be placed on the Internet for every company and financial institution in America. It is central that lenders, investors, creditors and business partners of companies and banks around the world completely understand where the risk resides in dealing with these individual companies.

Second: I would move for an immediate dissolution of the credit default swap market. Not only does the $65 trillion market bring enormous instability to the financial system, it has not been used as a hedging tool; instead, it is a purely speculative casino market.

In addition, the credit default swap market has created a level of interconnectedness between firms such that capitalism and its theory of creative destruction is no longer able to operate. Because of their interconnectedness in the credit default swap market, almost every major firm in the country is too big to fail because it will trigger massive other failures in the system. Capitalism does not work when companies are too big to fail. It certainly doesn't work when almost all big companies and banks are too big to fail.

It seems extreme to want to shut down the entire CDS market, but it was a mistake from the beginning. Simply having a common clearinghouse for trades or introducing some meaningless and ineffective regulation does not eliminate the fundamental problem that massive sharing of default risk between firms creates a collectivism closer to socialism than capitalism. Capitalism is dependent on individual initiative and the ability for individual firms to compete and fail. The credit default swap market's sharing of default risk across all firms has nationalized default risk, not unlike a Third World dictator nationalizing the means of production.

Third: I am praying that America is not fooled by the pundits and conservative columnists who tried to blame the current financial crisis solely on Washington and the government. Certainly, the government played a major role, but the primary reason for the crisis was deregulation. Yes, it was the government that deregulated business, but it was business that paid off the government through campaign contributions and lobbying efforts in order to become deregulated.

There is no way a free-market economy can work without regulation. It is a shame that we had to go through this enormous pain in order to see that. To many economists who have studied the importance of good institutions in creating economic growth, it was obvious that capitalism could not survive without proper rules, laws and regulation. Now hopefully we have all learned that lesson.

The challenge, of course, is for government to pass the right regulations. Again, as long as Wall Street and corporate America control our Congress through lobbying efforts, there is little hope that the meaningful regulations necessary to straighten out the markets will ever pass. Therefore, the third most fundamental change that has to happen and possibly the most difficult to accomplish, is that all corporate lobbying and campaign contributions in Washington must end.

Fourth: there is way too much leverage throughout the system. Individuals are going to have to reduce their leverage by defaulting on their debts. But when they default, it creates a loss at the banking institution that lent money to them. These losses are going to threaten the solvency of our entire banking system and will require the entire banking system to recapitalize and restructure, hopefully through a quick bankruptcy process so that the bank creditors will have to suffer along with US taxpayers.

The banks themselves are overly leveraged. Their leverage ratios of 25 to 1 or 35 to 1 debt-to-equity need to come down to more reasonable levels like 8 to 1 or 12 to 1. For this to happen, the banks have to dramatically shrink their balance sheets. You can see how painful it is going to be on the global economy if all the banks of the world sell half of their assets and make no new loans. I don't see any way that we can avoid this pain and loss and that is why I am so negative about the global economy's outlook for the next three to four years. This de-leveraging process is going to force governments, financial institutions, corporations and consumers, to quit making new purchases that stimulate the economy and instead to use monies to pay down old debts. It is good business practice, but it means that the GDP will have to contract.

Fifth: we need to get rid of complexity for complexity's sake. Mortgages should all be thirty-year fixed rate loans with at least 10 percent down payments. The derivatives market should be reexamined to see if its greater complexity is making the world safer or less stable.

Sixth: as we have seen in this text, there is a very serious principal agency problem in most of America's corporations and financial institutions. This needs to be seriously addressed. There are many middlemen in the investing process that also act as agents and do not necessarily have the investors' interest at heart. But the worst principal agent problem in the country right now is that management teams do not act with the shareholders' interest at heart. We must be smart enough to structure compensation agreements for managements so that they are more perfectly aligned to think like shareholders. I believe this means that we cannot pay large cash bonuses, big stock options and restricted stock grants each year to managements. Such bonus compensation and stock ownership will have to be earned over time and not paid out for five to ten years. That is the only way I can see to get managements to have the same long-term incentives as the shareholders. Management should not be motivated to grab quick profits that push up bonus pools and stock option values, but threaten the long-term solvency of their firms. And we have to make sure that boards of directors represent shareholders, not management.

Seventh: after all these calls for regulation, you might conclude that I'm a big government liberal. Nothing could be further from the truth. I hate big government. I blame our education problems on the fact that government runs our primary and secondary schools. I think we fail in wars because our government runs them. I think our Social Security and Medicare systems are bankrupt because they are part of government. I can't think of a single thing the government does well. I believe our Congress is a house of whores and our presidency is often sold to the highest bidder.

So I have no respect for government, especially big government. This puts me in quite a dilemma. You see, I don't trust big business to operate without rules and regulations, but I don't think the government is smart enough or independent enough from big business to write effective rules. I think they will write rules, but I don't think they'll be the right ones and I don't believe that the government will stay involved long enough to be sure they are implemented properly. George Stigler at the University of Chicago wrote his famous Nobel Prize-winning work showing that regulations do not hamper business, they help it. While the regulations are initially passed by activists interested in limiting business power, over time, the activists lose interest and the businesses themselves take over the regulatory bodies and use them to minimize competition and maximize profits.

So I have a completely different solution to this entire problem than increasing the size and power of the government and having it write more regulations for business. I don't trust them to do it effectively.

My solution — which is radical and at first you might find it hard to believe that we could accomplish it — is to downsize everything. Make everything smaller and less concentrated in power. Power corrupts and absolute power corrupts absolutely. We need to figure out a way in which the federal government is not so large and powerful that it can dictate terms to its own people and make them feel as if they are the slaves of their government instead of the government being the servants of the people. I believe this can be accomplished through a series of initiatives such as a greater emphasis on direct voting rather than representative voting, more emphasis on frequent polling of citizens and dramatically limiting the length of service of congressmen and senators in Washington.

Similarly, we need to limit the power of corporations that have gotten to be too big and too powerful. My suggestion is that every time a company becomes larger than $100 billion in market capitalization, including its debt, or attains greater than $300 billion in assets, the company should be broken up into two or three new companies. There is no dissolution of value because each shareholder would receive shares in each of the two or three new companies. But companies would not be allowed to grow to such a size that they can dictate terms to government or develop monopoly positions in the marketplace. This is the basis of how capitalism is supposed to work. Capitalism assumes that the agents participating in the market are completely independent and small enough that they cannot have an influence over the marketplace or over the regulations of the marketplace. Our largest banks and corporations clearly violate this basic tenet of capitalism.

I think putting the restriction on the size of companies — and it would need to be done globally through negotiations with other countries — would unleash a dramatic increase in entrepreneurship and innovation in this country. Could you imagine if, rather than just having three auto companies, thirty or forty years ago we had broken the Big Three in Detroit up into nine auto companies? I think that by now under this formula we would have had twenty to thirty automobile companies, each of them continually innovating and creating new products such as hybrid vehicles, hydrogen vehicles and electric vehicles. This type of innovation will happen in every industry naturally once we break up very large companies and prevent their muscle from allowing healthy innovation by smaller competitors.

That is my short list of the reforms I would like to see accomplished. I understand that these are major reforms, but you understand that this is a major crisis. We have come as close as any time in our lifetimes to a complete collapse of the global financial system and the world economy. I suggest that we not try this again. We need to accomplish these major changes to the way our capital markets and government are organized to ensure that this never happens again.

My outlook for the economy, as you can imagine, is not optimistic. As I said, I don't believe Obama will be successful in spending our way out of this recession. I also think this recession is far different than any short recession we have had in the past because of the tremendous leverage in the system that needs to be reduced and because of the structural problems in the way our capital markets are regulated that need to be addressed. We need to fundamentally change the way big business and big government work in this country. This crash has proved that the current system does not work and that minor adjustments will not help.

My prediction is that the economy will continue to trend downward for a number of years, not months. And rather than bouncing back as in past recessions, I believe that for a long period of time, five to eight years, the economy will struggle at a low level of output. The recovery will not be a V-shaped recovery, in which there is an instant bounce back, but more of an L recovery, in which we trade down and stay at a low output level for a long period of time.

There is also the very real risk, even though at this time it might be only 20 to 25 percent, that these warnings will be ignored, that Congress will continue to do the bidding of big corporations, that the American people will lose confidence in their financial markets and their government and that the entire system will collapse and we will head into a very real depression. Under this scenario there is no limit to how bad things might get. As I said earlier, I believe some 25 percent of Americans are already unemployed and this number could grow to 35 or 40 percent in a depression scenario.

If you are looking for stock price predictions, that is more difficult. I will say this. At 7,000 to 8,000, the stock market certainly has more downside than upside. It looks like the S&P 500 is going to earn approximately $50 in 2009 and if you assign a ten multiple to that, that gets you to an S&P valuation of 500. That is a further decline of about 35 percent from where the S&P is now. I cannot think of any upside scenario for stocks other than that they might temporarily improve under an Obama stimulus plan, but it will only be temporary.

I think that debt markets are certain to deteriorate. It makes no sense that a country with as much debt as the United States and with its trillions of dollars of annual operating deficits is able to borrow money at interest rates near zero percent. The rates that the US needs to pay in order to borrow funds are going to increase dramatically because inflation is going to come back. Inflation has to come back because the government will be printing money to fund all of these programs when people refuse to lend to us. When inflation comes back, interest rates will spike and those 2 percent ten-year Treasury bonds you bought will be worth about $.50 on the dollar.

While I believe commodity prices will continue to stay low, they will also increase in price as inflation returns. I would not recommend holding commodities because the real demand for them will decline as the economy softens, but the nominal price may increase as inflation reignites. The only place I would seek shelter from the storm with your investment funds is in gold and TIPS. Both of them will be good long-term protectors of your purchasing power, as they both do a very good job protecting against unexpected inflation.

As for housing prices, I believe they still have two or three more years to head down and they will not recover back to where they were. There is no way banks will be lending ten times your income for you to buy a house with no money down. Those days are gone. Under new, saner lending requirements and qualifications, housing prices will have to come down at least 30 percent nationwide from their peaks and more than 50 to 60 percent on the coasts, in California, Florida, Las Vegas and Arizona.

It has not been easy writing a book completely about lying. There were days during the writing of this book when the subject matter depressed me so much that I had to stop and take a break. I find it enormously disturbing that Americans, and now citizens of the world, are suffering very real hardships from a crisis that could easily have been avoided but for the lies of Wall Street, our biggest corporations and our government. It is estimated that an additional 200,000 to 400,000 babies in the world will die of malnutrition solely because of the malfeasance of big business and our government.

In closing, I know that we will never be successful in ending all lies. So my only advice is to be extremely careful who you trust. In financial dealings, always ask the question: What does this person who is advising me have to gain? Always try to understand what philosophical school the person comes from. If someone is an ardent libertarian, it doesn't make any difference what the facts are; they are going to suggest a solution that involves less government involvement. If you can identify their biases in advance it will help you understand their advice.

My very strong advice is to not accept lying in your personal and professional lives going forward. I believe that as a society, we have been much too forgiving of people who lie to us and cheat us. It will not stop until we make it so. Do not let liars and cheaters off the hook. Publicly call them on their unethical behavior and embarrass them. If it involves financial dealings, arrest them. But do not let them get away with it.

Truthfulness is not only the foundation of our society and a strong economic system, it is the basis of all human interaction and organization, and without it, life can seem purposeless and unfulfilling.

And now the hardest advice of all. Let us stop lying to each other. Lying is not a victimless crime. Lying causes real suffering and hardship. Let's do all we can to make our lives a search for the truth, and in so doing truly inspire others to lead more fulfilling and ethical lives.

Chapter 9

Written in July 2009

Selected Excerpts from "Who Caused the Economic Crisis?"

Following are selected excerpts from a series of three articles that were originally published by salon.com in July 2009.

Simon Johnson, the former chief economist of the International Monetary Fund (IMF), is the cofounder of BaselineScenario.com, a Web site tracking the ongoing financial crisis. He is also the Ronald A. Kurtz professor of entrepreneurship at the MIT Sloan School of Management.

From June to July of 2009, Talbott and Johnson held a series of e-mail conversations on the following topic: "The economic crisis: Who caused it? Was it preventable? Was criminal activity involved in bringing it about? And is it over?"

Below are Talbott's emails to Johnson.

From: John Talbott
To: Simon Johnson
Subject: A Vast Criminal Enterprise

Simon,

I believe economists are doing a very poor job of explaining to the American people who and what caused the current economic crisis. I think the reasons for this are threefold.

One: Economists and media pundits -- themselves mostly gentlemanly elites anxious to please corporate America -- are slow to make the accusation that what happened here was truly criminal and so miss the real story. The American people understand that when a group of bankers shuffle some paper unproductively and get away with hundreds of billions of dollars in bonuses, yet cause a loss of $40 trillion in global wealth and cause approximately 100 million people to become unemployed worldwide, there is only one word to describe it: criminal. We don't have to argue about whether their actions were technically illegal or violated existing statutes, as in this conspiracy the crooks were writing their own regulations and legislation through their control of the government by lobbying.

Two: There has been no criminal investigation to date, so evidence supporting criminality has not been uncovered -- no one is looking for it. Liberals hate to think that Obama, led by Geithner and Summers, is part of a grand cover-up scheme, but that is exactly what is going on. How else can you explain the lack of criminal investigations? Why isn't the FBI breaking down the doors of the commercial and investment banks and grabbing computers so as to preserve incendiary e-mails that will most definitely implicate executives? Why are managements that caused this still in their jobs and still receiving bonuses? Are the bonuses paid to the folks at AIG that caused its collapse nothing more than hush money? How can the rating agencies still be in business? Why don't we make one arrest and lean on the bankster to see if he will fold like the cheap suit that he is and name other conspirators? The FBI spends more time investigating $2,000 drug buys than they have to date investigating the biggest heist in the history of the world: $40 trillion, that's trillion with a T, that's 40 million bags each containing $1 million.

The third reason that we have not had an easy-to-understand explanation from economists as to the cause of this mess: I think we're all trying to fit the facts as we know them into one simple story of causation. I believe there are actually three different storylines occurring contemporaneously, and all of them criminal. It is similar to what Winston Churchill said about trying to forecast Russia's next moves in 1939: "It is a riddle, wrapped in a mystery, inside an enigma."

So what are these three criminal storylines? The first, and the smallest (if you can believe it) at approximately $10 trillion, is the housing crash and the mortgage meltdown. Totally criminal, as its primary cause was banksters stuffing worthless mortgage paper into CDOs [securities known as collateralized debt obligations] and calling them AAA. Criminal at every level, as real estate agents were convincing their buyers to pay more, not less, to "earn" their fees through a winning bid, appraisers were offering non-independent and completely tainted appraisals, mortgage brokers were altering loan documents and changing income data to qualify buyers, bankers were paying rating agencies to call junk paper AAA and principal investors like pension funds, insurance companies and sovereign governments

158

failed to perform even the minimum levels of due diligence demanded by their fiduciary duties.

. But the second story is even bigger and extends far beyond mortgages to the entire banking system. The banks had found a way to avoid the regulation that everyone knew they needed ever since they were given federally backed depositor insurance to prevent bank runs back in the '30s. They became one of the biggest lobbyists and campaign contributors to your Congress and your presidents. Then, amazingly, they just asked that all limitations on their activities be removed -- and they were. If I paid you $2 for your vote, it would be illegal, but somehow these banks could pay hundreds of millions to our congressmen and presidents for their votes and it was all perfectly legal. Completely nuts!

So what did banks do that was criminal? Well, first they paid your government to eliminate bank restrictions, then they overleveraged, knowing they could not honor contracts with such leverage, then they lied to their shareholders about the risks and magnitudes of their positions, hid their positions illegally off balance sheet and through the use of derivatives managed to violate minimum capital requirements on an almost daily basis. They took bank debt leverage from 8:1 to over 30:1, thus assuring that the banking system could not survive even a modest credit tightening or recession. They made crazy bets in the credit default swap market that they could never honor in a downturn. They loaned money to anyone who could fog a knife because they knew they were going to stuff it to others through securitization and CDOs. If we had a criminal investigation, we would have access to the incriminating phone calls and e-mails in which the banksters disclosed what they really thought of the assets they were pawning off on others. To see how traders incriminate themselves, watch "The Smartest Guys in the Room," about Enron's collapse.

The final storyline of criminality is the biggest of all. It is bigger than the current financial crisis. It is corporate America's complete control of our nation's elected officials, especially our Congress, through lobbying and campaign donations. Yes, the banks played this game, but the game was much bigger than just the financial industry. Coal-fired utilities have so watered down impending legislation concerning global warming that they have now come out in favor of it in the House vote. TARP money went to banking friends of Hank Paulson, although 97 percent of congressional correspondence from the American people was against it. The credit card industry took a minor slap on the wrist, but faces no limitation on the egregious interest rates it can charge its customers. Pharmaceutical and hospital corporations are fighting hard to keep Americans from having a public alternative to their healthcare and right now are winning that fight. The transportation industry is at the government trough trying to pass a $500 billion windfall. The AARP prevents any meaningful reform of Social Security; the teachers' union does the same for education reform. Is it crazy to think that defense companies like Dick Cheney's Halliburton (which saw its stock price increase 600 percent during the Iraq war, thanks to no-bid contracts) may be promoting U.S. aggression around the world?

The American people understand that their government is corrupt; that is why they don't want to rely solely on more government regulation to solve this crisis. No, if we are to ever to see positive growth again in this country, we need to make the fundamental reforms that are necessary without relying on regulation which is so often co-opted or captured by those we are trying to regulate. This suggests we need to find a way to get corporations out of our government and ensure they never become either too big to fail or so big that they improperly influence markets and our government.

John

From: John Talbott
To: Simon Johnson
Subject: Complexity With No Purpose

Simon,

Don't worry, this isn't over yet. We haven't missed our chance to enact real reform. There isn't going to be any big recovery until we address these fundamental issues. Given the debt overhang, the banks' general unwillingness to lend, the lack of transparency and trust in the markets, the possible change in people's desire for increased status-seeking through crazy borrowing and crazy consumption, a substantial decline in immigration and population growth and the fast approaching retirement of the baby boomers, I don't see the American economy growing in real terms for years, if not decades, into the future. The real risk is that the economy will continue to suffer, unemployment will increase and discontent will grow to the point that the Republicans stage a comeback. It may sound far-fetched now, but I can tell you: There is enormous anger out there about government spending, the increased debt, the bailouts and the fact that

Washington is still taking orders from special interests. This is not the change people signed on for.

You are right -- this is much bigger than Bernie Madoff and his friends stealing billions from investors. Because the banks lobbied to change the law before they acted, their actions are technically legal. But paying elected representatives money to change laws so that you can violate them seems to me to be at the heart of what criminal activity is all about. But you are right, because the laws were changed, criminal prosecutors in the states are not going to be very effective in bringing effective prosecutions, especially given that federal enforcement agencies like the FBI and the SEC [Securities and Exchange Commission] are collecting so little useful evidence and pursuing so few leads.

It is a real question how a country can stop corruption once corruption reaches its legislature, since the legislature is the place where we would expect reform legislation to be enacted. I believe this is one of the reasons why the poorest countries of the world have remained poor for centuries. As we have seen here in the U.S., once you lose control of your legislature, accomplishing real reform is a much bigger problem. Prosecuting attorneys are not going to be much help, judges and the court system have their hands tied by corrupt legislation and well-meaning presidents face ostracism inside the Beltway if they openly oppose Congress, lobbyists and corporate special interests.

I believe pressure for reform has to come directly from the people. And I believe that Washington is so corrupt that attempts to bring reform through the vote will be ineffectual. The two parties have too much of a lock on power while incumbents have too much money (and they have gerrymandered their districts to the point that their losing is near impossible). Congress' approval rating of 14 percent and congressional incumbents' 98.4 percent success rate at re-election fully describes the problem of attempting reform through the vote.

The task is getting Americans organized, because once organized we hold the ultimate trump card. It is we Americans who make these corporations what they are today by buying their products and services. Any threat to not buy the products of big government lobbyists would certainly get their attention. I honestly believe it is also in the interest of our biggest corporations to stop influencing our government, because until they do, our country is not going to be seeing any real economic growth. Banksters, greedy healthcare companies, a weak education system, unnecessary wars and a bankrupt government trying to fund its retirees' costs are not conducive to economic growth and the corporations should come to realize this. This is a classic collective-action problem where each corporation cheats and steals a little, but the overall effect is to strangle the economy and prevent a truly prosperous future.

Of course, the real reforms that need to be accomplished, once we get corporations out of Washington and politics, include limiting the leverage of banks and prohibiting them from risky activities -- principal trading for their own account, derivatives trading and many other investment banking activities -- and assuring complete transparency of all of their positions. We also need to strengthen the board supervision of management by getting managers, including the CEO and his cronies, out of the boardroom and replacing them with real shareholder representatives. We don't need to limit compensation, but we need to make sure that it is structured so that toxic waste cannot be left behind by a poorly thought-out bonus system.

But there are bigger reforms that are also needed. We need to downsize all corporations, especially the banks. We need to make sure they are not too big to fail. This downsizing will not hurt investors, as they will get two new smaller company shares of equal worth for every big old company share they held.

We need to shut down the credit default swap (CDS) market, because extensive trading of default risk makes everyone too interconnected to fail. I know the CDS market was created to limit risk through hedging, but it has done just the opposite. It has made all firms so interconnected that one cannot fail without bringing them all down. This violates the first rule of capitalism -- that firms must be allowed to fail -- and therefore it needs to be stopped completely. The only analogy I can think of to demonstrate how crazy this market has become is to go back in history to the early days of risk sharing when well-capitalized institutions on shore offered insurance against the loss of a ship at sea. The CDS market, if it were operating back then, would have allowed ships at sea themselves to guarantee the fate of other ships at sea, with very small boats such as hedge funds somehow insuring the return of very large merchant ships. The whole mess would have become so interconnected that one ship's sinking would have bankrupted everybody.

People today seem to think that just because two people want to trade something, it must be good. Because the CDS market is big, it must be useful, goes the argument. It gets at the belief system that you suggested people have adopted: that markets are inherently good.

Maybe always efficient, but not always good. There are some things like company default risk that shouldn't be traded. In the past people wanted to buy and sell slaves, child pornography, women's bodies, weapons of mass destruction or to offer payments to elected government representatives and bribes to international governments and competitors. Just because a market can develop does not mean the functioning of that market is good for society. Markets cannot self-reflect. That is what humans do. Only we can decide if a particular market is doing more harm than good.

I would extend my reforms to include shutting down most derivatives trading. If used properly, it can be an effective hedging tool, but since its introduction it has made investment analysis moot as no one actually knows what risks you are buying when you buy the stock of a company or bank actively engaged in derivatives. You may be bullish on gold prices, so you buy a gold mining stock -- only to find out that the company has in fact hedged its gold exposure so effectively through derivatives that it makes money only if gold prices decline, not increase.

Similarly, I would shut down the hedge fund industry. They are nothing more than enablers for these banks and companies like AIG to concoct schemes to avoid regulation or increase risk. Basic investment theory says you can't beat the markets, so I will bet that the hedge funds that are claiming to do so are doing it illegally through insider trading and market manipulation of individual stocks and asset prices. Don't take my word for it. Let's have the government tap the phones and check the e-mails of the hedge funds for a six-month period on a confidential basis and see what happens to their reported outsized profitability and trading brilliance.

John

From: John Talbott
To: Simon Johnson
Subject: Taking Back the Country

I think you and I and most economists suffer from an antiquated belief that if we can just figure out exactly what went wrong, policymakers will beat a path to our door to ask our help in enacting necessary reforms. Unfortunately, the world no longer works that way. Our corrupted government, our criminal businesses and banking institutions, lobbyists, special interests and the corporate controlled media are not interested in fixing this problem. They are making trillions of dollars through a vast scheme that transfers wealth from ordinary American taxpayers and consumers to their corrupt coffers. You are right that if big business thought about it, they should support efforts at restricting lobbying so that growth-oriented government policies could be implemented without the influence of corrupting special interests. But each lobbying corporation is also its own special interest and so such internal reform is impossible.

The million-dollar question is: Why haven't ordinary Americans reacted more passionately and angrily in taking real action to end this systemic abuse? A decade ago, I wrote my first book on the corrupting influence of big business lobbying on our government and concluded at the time that average Americans would not focus on the issue until they had suffered real pain. I concluded that you can't defuse a bomb in America until after it has gone off.

But now the bomb has exploded. Four million Americans are unemployed, millions have lost their homes and most have taken a very substantial hit to their incomes, retirement savings and wealth. Why aren't Americans in the streets protesting this corrupt, enormously damaging criminal enterprise? I have traveled enough around America to realize that even though the current situation is enormously complex and not all Americans can describe exactly how the CDO market works, almost without exception every American can relate to you his frustration with how corrupt this government is and how unjust corporate lobbying and special influence in Washington has become. They get it. As a matter of fact, some of my high school-educated friends from my home state of Kentucky understand it a lot better than my Harvard-educated friends from Wall Street.

So I don't think the current challenge is figuring out exactly what caused the crisis. Focusing on what caused this episode will lead to narrow regulatory reform that reminds me that we all now take off our shoes at airports because one crazy fellow had the idea of putting a bomb in his heel. So while reform is needed in subprime mortgages, securitization, derivatives and even in the magnitude of our financial institutions, none of these get at the fundamental problem: The people of this country are no longer making the rules by which they wish to live. If subprime mortgages hadn't blown up, some other area of highly leveraged bank lending would have eventually imploded. Even if the banking industry hadn't crashed, some other sector of the corrupt business/government criminal enterprise would have. Maybe the ice shelf of Greenland would have collapsed into the North Atlantic, maybe we would have run out of oil, maybe Microsoft's monopoly position in operating systems would have led to a worldwide computer virus shutdown, maybe poor consumer safety standards with China would have led to a global disease epidemic. The point is that when corporations make the rules, the results are not always good for the inhabitants of the planet.

So we don't have to decide today exactly what the reforms will be -- we just need to get corporate America out of our government so that the people can deliberate and make these reform decisions themselves without undue influence from bankers and corporations.

But there are two huge impediments to accomplishing this. This is not a traditional economics problem; it is an organizing problem or a collective action problem. People know the system is rigged and broken and unjust, but they feel as if there is very little that any one of them can do to effect much change. The organizing task is further complicated by the fact that our media, including television networks, cable TV, radio, newspapers and magazine and book publishing, are almost all sponsored, owned and controlled by big corporations. The only hope is the Internet, over which big business has tried, but to date, failed to successfully exert its dominance. The Internet will prove to be both a source of unbiased news and information as well as the communication tool concerned citizens can utilize to fight back against big government, big business and big media.

What has to happen to get this movement started? First, I think people need to see that there is a channel being constructed that has the potential to effective in directing their anger into real positive reform and change. Next, people have to believe that if they invest their time in such an effort they have the potential of winning.

It is time for Americans to realize that things are not going to improve until they get involved. It will take time. But the economy is not going to improve until we straighten out our corrupt system. Do you have anything more important that you are working on than this? The survival of liberal democratic society in the world.

Chapter 10

Written in May 2010

"The Trillion Dollar Fraud"

Originally published on salon.com on May 1, 2010.

Commercial banks, by law, have to hold a certain percentage of their deposits as cash at the Federal Reserve. From January 1959 until August 2008, the total of these reserves held by the commercial banks at the Fed grew from $11.1 billion to $46.2 billion. At no time during this almost 50-year period did the total bank reserves held at the Fed exceed the minimum required by law by more than $2 billion.

But since August 2008, these bank reserves held at the Fed have exploded to more than $1.2 trillion (as of March 2010), even though only $65.6 billion was required to be deposited by law.

This increase in excess reserves resulted directly from the Fed's policy of dramatically increasing the quantity (and lowering the quality threshold) of assets it bought in the marketplace. During the past 20 months, the Fed has tripled the size of its balance sheet by acquiring more than $1.5 trillion of new assets, more than $1 trillion of which are mortgage-backed securities.

What is going on here? Why would commercial banks hold $1 trillion more than they legally had to in reserves at the Fed, earning only 0.25 percent interest per year and why would the Fed buy more than $1 trillion of mortgage securities of undisclosed quality in the marketplace?

If you recall, back in 2008, Hank Paulson, our treasury secretary at the time, convinced Congress over a weekend that he needed $700 billion of TARP funds to get the toxic assets off our commercial banks' books. Amazingly, within weeks of being given the funds by Congress, Paulson decided not to proceed with the purchase of toxic assets from the banks, instead giving away hundreds of billions of dollars to the commercial and investment banks and funding a series of bailouts — giving money to Chrysler, General Motors and AIG (some of which immediately found its way back to the commercial and investment banking community).

At the time, nobody explained what happened to the toxic assets on the banks' books whose purchase was the original stated purpose of TARP. We now know that the financial crisis was not caused solely by a liquidity crunch or an irrational loss of confidence, but rather by the fact that the marketplace realized that the commercial banks held more than a trillion dollars of very poor-quality assets, mostly mortgage securities such as collateralized debt obligations or CDOs and that these bad assets were sizable enough to bankrupt even our biggest banks. How bad? Even the AAA tranche of the typical CDO is facing a mortgage default rate of approximately 93 percent today.

I believe the reason Paulson didn't pursue his original toxic-asset purchasing plan is because such a purchase would have created a market price for these assets and then all of the banks would have had to mark their poor-quality assets to this low market price. This would have resulted in the bankruptcy of almost all the major commercial and investment banks because their leverage was so high that they couldn't withstand such a hit to their equity.

When Paulson couldn't achieve one of his objectives during the crisis, he typically called on Ben Bernanke to see if the Fed could be of assistance. Paulson was in a difficult position and needed Bernanke's help. He had, just two weeks earlier, told Congress that if they didn't approve TARP and deal with the banks' toxic assets, the entire financial system would collapse. Now he was about to be exposed as either a liar or just completely wrongheaded, because the toxic assets were still on the banks' books and he was using TARP money elsewhere. What I believe the Fed did next was fraudulent and deceitful, its full impact still hidden from the American public, who want bank reform.

The Fed, I am convinced, went to these commercial banks and offered to take many of their toxic mortgage assets off their books, often accepting them as collateral for loans to the banks. In exchange, the Fed credited the commercial banks with an increase in the reserves held at the Fed, so long as the banks agreed not to withdraw the excess reserves immediately. Magically, the Fed was able to take a bad asset like a CDO and transform it into a sparkling good asset: bank reserves at the Fed. The irony is that the CDO itself began as a compilation of leaden BBB subprime mortgages and had been transformed into a golden AAA security only through the alchemy of the CDO process. And I think the record will show that the Fed intentionally overpaid for these securities, so that the banks wouldn't have to acknowledge life-threatening losses on the sales or the remarking of their inventory of similar assets. The Fed also began buying mortgage securities directly in the marketplace in an attempt to create demand in the absence of a healthy securitization program.

So the Federal Reserve, with no approval by the president, the Congress, the people or their elected representatives, ended up purchasing $1.5 trillion of new assets of unknown quality. The Fed is controlled by our nation's banks and so it shouldn't surprise us when it uses taxpayer money to save these very same commercial banks.

What concerns many knowledgeable investors is that the Fed doesn't have the money needed to purchase these assets and instead prints new money. As of March 2010, there was approximately $1 trillion of currency outstanding in the country, not including the more than $1 trillion of bank reserves at the Fed. So if the Fed doesn't shrink its balance sheet, we can expect inflation to come roaring back as banks increase lending in the future.

Some have suggested that the Fed is well-aware of this problem and is reviewing creative, if not necessarily transparent, methods to take care of it. Bernanke has said that he is opposed to the outright sale of these assets in the marketplace. One rumor is that the Fed is looking at selling more than $1 trillion of mortgage securities back to Fannie Mae and Freddie Mac. This would complete the circle of deceit, because Fannie and Freddie could fund their purchase with increased borrowings guaranteed by the government, which wouldn't show up on the government's balance sheet because Fannie and Freddie aren't consolidated entities of the federal government (even though they are now owned by the government). Total government debt would increase by $1 trillion, but it would be hidden from the taxpayer, off the balance sheet. The plan has the added advantage of the Fed never having to recognize the losses on any toxic assets included in the transfer, as Congress has already said it will commit unlimited resources to fund any future losses at Fannie or Freddie. Fannie and Freddie are the ideal places for toxic assets to go to die.

A second idea being discussed is for the Treasury, over time, to slowly transfer real money to the Fed to reduce these excess reserve balances and thus cover any resulting undisclosed losses in the portfolio. Of course, such transfers would have to be funded with increased Treasury debt.

No one knows how many of the $1.5 trillion of securities that the Fed has purchased are toxic or what decline in value they have suffered. The House of Representatives passed legislation requiring a regular audit of the Fed's assets, but this provision was removed by Chris Dodd, D-Conn. in the financial reform package currently being debated in the Senate, for good reason if I'm right about all of this. A number of amendments to the bill are currently being discussed, including Bernie Sanders' amendment to include a required audit of the Fed. As Friday's Wall Street Journal noted: "Obama administration officials have declined to weigh in on any specific amendments, with one exception: a move by Sen. Bernie Sanders (I., Vt.) to give the government more power to audit certain operations at the Federal Reserve. Fed and administration officials have signaled they would fight to stop it at all costs."

We all want stability in our financial system, but we also want transparency in our government. It is undemocratic to allow one institution, the Federal Reserve, overwhelmingly controlled by the commercial banks that it is supposed to be regulating, to make such critical decisions about which commercial banks will fail and which will be allowed to survive — and how much of the taxpayers' money will be used for all of it. The Fed exceeded its original mandate and acted clandestinely and deceitfully and because of this, American taxpayers face an additional cost of up to $1 trillion that they and their representatives never agreed to undertake.

Chapter 11

Written in May 2010

"Who Are the Real Winners in Europe's Bailout?"

Originally published on salon.com on May 11. 2010.

On Sunday, the European Union and the International Monetary Fund announced they were creating a $955 billion fund to rescue euro zone economies that find themselves in financial peril. This announcement came less than five days after the EU had decided to make $140 billion available to Greece to aid in its recovery.

What few people realize is that the banks holding a substantial portion of Greece's $430 billion of government debt are not being asked to take a single dollar haircut to their investment. This is highly unusual for restructurings that involve the IMF. Typically, to receive IMF funding, a country must engage in not only budgetary and fiscal tightening, but also haircuts to the banks and other debt investors. The idea that companies and countries can restructure without debt investors losing a penny is a relatively new phenomenon. Hank Paulson and Ben Bernanke pretty much invented it when they bailed out Fannie Mae and Freddie Mac, Bear Stearns, Citibank, Goldman Sachs, Morgan Stanley, Merrill Lynch, Bank of America, Morgan Guaranty and AIG and assured that all of their creditors were paid off at 100 cents on the dollar. And the Greek government debt works out to almost $170,000 per household, which, by definition, is unsustainable and needs restructuring.

People may think that the beneficiaries of this EU largess are the poorer countries of Europe and their people, who have suffered through high unemployment and domestic economies weakened by the crisis. But if the banks' lending to countries such as Greece, Portugal, Ireland, Spain and Italy are going to be repaid in full from the proceeds of these EU and IMF programs, then maybe we need to rethink who actually is benefiting from these programs. This is not lost on the people of Greece, 100,000 of whom took to the streets last week to protest cuts in their government's budget, which was part of the

Greek bailout plan. Nor is it lost on Wall Street: on Monday, European bank stocks shot up an average of 20 percent -- a sign that traders are well aware of who the primary beneficiaries of the bailout plan will be.

At first blush, it does appear that some of these poorer European nations have significant amounts of government debt and are running fairly large annual budget deficits. Following are the levels of government debt for a selection of countries, mostly of the Organisation for Economic Cooperation and Development (OECD), expressed as a percentage of each country's GDP:

Government debt as a percentage of GDP

Japan 195
Greece 133
Belgium 124
Italy 116
Portugal 78
Austria 74
France 70
Denmark 60
Netherlands 60
India 60
United Kingdom 56
United States 53
Hungary 52
Finland 49
Sweden 49
Brazil 47
Germany 46
Iceland 45
Ireland 38
Spain 35
Switzerland 32
Canada 29
Poland 29
Turkey 25
Czech Republic 25
Slovak Republic 21
Slovenia 19
Luxembourg 11
Australia 7

Investors become concerned when government debt exceeds 100 percent of GDP, which explains Greece's and Italy's predicaments.

Portugal is right behind them. But based solely on current debt levels, it's not clear what the investors' concerns are about Ireland and Spain. I also can't explain Japan's poor debt ranking, other than to say that it looks completely unsustainable.

Of course, current country debt levels do not tell the full story as to which countries are most at risk of defaulting. Annual government budget deficits are also important because they can add annually to the country's debt burden. Similarly, expected growth rates of GDP are very important because as troubled countries' economies shrink, their debt loads become ever more burdensome.

Europe's problems are not limited solely to Greece, Portugal, Ireland, Spain and Italy. These five countries in total owe $1 trillion to France and their banks, they owe Germany $700 billion and they owe Britain $400 billion -- not to mention the money they owe the Swiss and U.S. banks. If these five countries were to default, the problem would quickly shift to the richest nations of Europe. This is the real reason for the announced bailouts. And it is not just the wealthier countries' banks that are being bailed out here; the governments of some wealthier European countries would themselves come under great financial pressure if these loans were not repaid, since they would then have to deal with enormous losses in their own banking sectors.

If the banks in these wealthier European nations were to suffer substantial losses from their sovereign debt investments, you can be sure that their governments would try to bail them out and make them whole. But this may not be as easy as it seems. It turns out that the size of the banking systems in many wealthier European countries far exceeds the total GDP of the country. Here is some summary data for the countries (most of them OECD members) in which the total of all bank assets exceed 100 percent of GDP.

Bank assets as a percentage of GDP

Luxembourg 2,461
Ireland 872
Switzerland 723
Denmark 477
Iceland 458
Netherlands 432
United Kingdom 389
Belgium 380
Sweden 340

France 338
Austria 299
Spain 251
Germany 246
Finland 205
Australia 205
Portugal 188
Canada 157
Italy 151
Greece 141

(For comparison, total banking assets in the U.S. are equal to approximately 82 percent of GDP.)

It's now obvious why Ireland is included in the troubled country category: Its banks assets are close to nine times as big as its total GDP and all banks across Europe face substantial losses to their loan portfolios. Certainly real estate investments and sovereign credit investing will remain trouble for the banks, but as the recession and unemployment linger, consumer and corporate lending will also become problematic to the banks.

Switzerland has banks with assets of more than seven times its GDP. For the United Kingdom, banks have close to four times as much in assets as the GDP. And in France, Austria, Sweden, Belgium, the Netherlands and Denmark, the ratios are all between 3- and 5-to-1. Certainly, one can see that if the troubled nations of Europe, like Greece, fail to repay their loans to these banks in full, not only would the banks get in trouble, but these very large wealthy nations could quickly find themselves with an insurmountable problem on their books.

This situation is all very similar to the subprime mortgage crisis that started in the United States in 2007. In both cases, European banks bought what they thought were AAA assets; CDO tranches and sovereign debt, only to find out that the ratings were terribly overstated. AAA tranches of some CDOs are now experiencing 93 percent default rates.

In each case, the rating agencies played an important and conspiratorial role in labeling many CDO securities and most sovereign credits as AAA. This is important because banks in Europe are now able to hold such AAA securities on their balance sheets with little to no capital reserves held against them. In essence, this means that the banks can hold these AAA assets with infinite leverage. And that is pretty much what they've done: the leverage of these European banks sometimes exceeds 35- or 40-to-1.

So in both the subprime crisis and now the sovereign debt crisis, the banks loaned too much money to inferior debtors with too much bank leverage based solely on the opinion of a rating agency. Clearly, the bank that over-lent was more at fault than either the homeowner or the borrowing country. In both cases, the homeowner and the government of the sovereign nation may have done stupid things with the money, but the real stupidity was the bank's lending in the first place. Clearly, if anyone should be blamed for these crises, it's the banks that over-lent -- and therefore it is the banks that should suffer most of the pain in restructuring. If I were advising Greece, I would tell it to default on its debts and force its creditors to take an 85 percent haircut. This would put the true cost of the crisis on those most responsible -- the banks, not the people of Greece.

If you want to predict which countries of Europe face possible default risk in the future, it's not enough to just look at current levels of government debt. I have created a forecast of how bad things might get for the countries of Europe by looking at a hypothetical future in which the governments are forced to make their own banks whole on losses equal to 10 percent of total bank assets by country. This might seem like an extreme loss scenario until you realize that Citibank has already been made whole on 15 percent of its assets by guarantees from the U.S. government and that people are expecting Fannie Mae and Freddie Mac to realize losses of more than 20 percent of their total assets before their restructuring is complete.

In addition, I assumed very little real growth for these countries in the future, which is reasonable because they have to deal with this banking and government crisis and because their citizens are aging rapidly and they are losing valuable members of their labor force to retirement. To account for increases in future debt loads due to ongoing government deficits, I took each country's current annual deficit, multiplied by seven and added it to the country's total debt. The following table is an estimate of how bad things might get in the near future for the countries that end up with more than 100 percent of their GDP in government debt under this formulation.

Possible future government debt loads as a percentage of GDP with 10 percent bank asset losses assumed

Luxembourg 287
Japan 262
Greece 215
Ireland 210
Belgium 201
United Kingdom 188
Italy 169
France 164
Iceland 162
Portugal 150
Denmark 146
Netherlands 145
Austria 142
United States 136
India 133
Spain 120
Switzerland 114
Germany 108
Sweden 104
Finland 103

It is apparent that Greece, Ireland, Italy and Portugal are all troubled and face real default risks. Spain, less so. But it is also apparent that some of the largest countries of the world will also face very severe consequences in trying to repair their banks' balance sheets. I don't see how Japan can escape this fate given that its debt, seen here, will be close to triple the size of its GDP. Similarly, Luxembourg, the United Kingdom, France, Iceland, Denmark, the Netherlands, Austria and the United States are at severe risk of getting into financial trouble as a direct result of these banking crises.

In 2008, I wrote a book titled "Contagion," in which I warned that the subprime mortgage crisis that started in the U.S. would spread to prime mortgages, infect the financial stability of the largest city and state governments in the U.S. and eventually spread to impact most of the nations of the world, especially in Europe. This latest sovereign debt crisis adds fuel to that fire. The solution cannot continue to be the bailouts of banks at 100 cents on the dollar at the expense of taxpayers and citizens. A debt crisis cannot be solved with more debt. We must find a way to reduce the debt levels of all banks, corporations, citizens and countries so that we are better poised for real growth and prosperity in the future.

Chapter 12

Written in June 2010

"The Failure of Financial Reform - Itemized"

Originally published on huffingtonpost.com on June 30, 2010.

It is really quite incredible that of all the things that went wrong to cause the latest economic crisis, the new financial reform bill does almost nothing with regards to the following key issues. Here are the original problems and the actions being taken.

1. Bank leverage: Very little is done about this in the new bill -- banks still can do things off balance sheet (what is the business purpose of doing things off balance sheet except to deceive? [Alex Talbott]) -- still using risk measurements based on historical volatility of assets, VAR, which can easily be gamed by managements rather than strict capital requirements based on actual ratios to real equity book capital. Needs to get from 35 to one before crisis to proposed 20 to one under this legislation, but really should be below 8 to one. Larry Kotlikoff of Boston University suggests one to one is the right ratio and calls the concept Limited Purpose Banking (LPB). Without bank leverage, it is hard to imagine how a small regional economic downturn in say, Houston oil markets or Silicon Valley's semiconductor industry could ever spread contagiously nationally or internationally, thus stopping most recessions and depressions before they start.

2- Interest rates too low: Even lower today.

3- Lobbying and money in politics: Even worse today having been blessed by Supreme Court that corporations can fund campaign advertising directly and financial firms have stepped up with big donations and lobbying effort to stymie the reform bill itself.

4- Too much debt everywhere: Now, more, especially on local and federal governments including Europe and Japan and global banks. Banks slow to deleverage and consumers are not spending substantially less and saving more, they are just defaulting on their debts to lessen their debt loads.

5- Depositor insurance: Disguised as a benefit to depositors, it is actually a windfall to lower funding costs of banks and encourages stupid behavior by them because of the moral hazard with regard to riskiness of assets held, businesses entered and leverage undertaken. Increased permanently from $100K to $250K per account since crisis.

6- Bank consumer fees: Much higher now. Consumers and taxpayers are basically paying for a problem they had nothing to do with in creating. This was solely a banking and government problem. To blame homebuyers for accepting a no money down, 100% home loan at 2% per year to buy a home they never in their wildest dreams thought they could afford ignores the mistakes the banks made in offering these terms. Once you offer someone 100% financing, it is no longer his problem, it is yours. Individual home owners did not buy these properties, they were actually owned by the banks and their investors who put up all the money.

7- Predatory lending: Still active. Listen to the pitch for reverse mortgages to our seniors on television and try to explain how they actually work or try to calculate how much profit spread the banks have built into those transactions for themselves, then imagine having a touch of Alzheimer's and doing it correctly.

8- Global investor diversification: No change, investors encouraged to hold thousands of assets around the world through mutual funds, index funds or well diversified institutional funds making supervision of managements impossible and encouraging the hiring of too many financial intermediaries and consultants as supposed experts.

9- Credit Default Swap (CDS) market: Was the prime reason everyone was too interconnected to fail as one domino sent them all crashing. Nothing new to report as they either need to be shut down or regulated like insurance companies because that is what they are. Should be shut down because they create too much systemic counterparty risk that can crash the entire system, but at a minimum, you should not be able to buy CDSs naked, only as a hedge against a similar asset. It makes no sense to buy a company or its debt, buy CDS default insurance equal in value to a hundred times what you paid for the company and then drive the company into bankruptcy, regardless of its financial health. This is the equivalent of buying fire insurance on your neighbor's home and then lighting the arson yourself.

10- Criminal behavior: Banksters, realtors, appraisers, mortgage brokers, investment bankers all broke the law with their fraudulent and criminal and conspiratorial acts and many private and public funds failed to perform their fiduciary duties or required investment due diligence. The scale of the criminal enterprise is vast crossing many industries and country borders and the damages incalculable as globally we have lost over 50 million jobs, 20 million have lost their homes, $20 trillion of savings has been permanently lost to investors and more than 100 million people have been thrown back into the destitution and poverty of earning less than$2 a day. No arrests, no yellow crime scene tape around Goldman's new office building, no seizing of computers and emails and phone records of the suspected banksters and their lawyers and accountants. Certainly, many congressmen should be imprisoned for taking bribes disguised as campaign donations that encouraged them to remove or ignore important financial oversight regulations, but since they write the laws I doubt this will ever happen.

11- Board control: Still dominated by CEO and company insiders and their friends as opposed to being controlled by shareholders directly. Get the CEO and other corporate executives completely out of the boardroom which should be run exclusively by genuine shareholder representatives.

12- Securitization: Little changed, talk of issuer having to hold 5% of securities issued, but this is still subject to how final regulation is written. Securitization market is dead until they straighten out the rigged ratings game and re-instill investors trust in banks and investment banks who purposely packaged the worst trash they had on their books, gift wrapped it as a CDO and laid it off on many of their biggest and best clients.

13- Ratings agencies: Reform ignored fundamental problem with issuers paying for ratings rather than investors.

14- Fannie Mae and Freddie Mac: So far, no change, their restructuring was not included in this bill, they are still making loans of which many are going to turn out bad as they are one of only a few institutions lending into areas that are experiencing steep price declines currently and the best predictor of future default is home price declines in a region.

15- Too many financial middlemen: Because of overemphasis on diversification, investors, both individual and institutional, hold such far flung and complex investments that they become overly dependent on a long list of financial advisors and consultants and managers. At best these advisors have different motivations than the primary investor, don't care as much about protecting against losses since it isn't their money and increases the risk of fraudulent and criminal behavior somewhere in the long and complex investment food chain.

16- Who regulates?: Very little change, same guys in congress and at the Fed, Treasury and the FDIC who got us into this mess.

17- To big to fail (TBTF): Has gotten worse as the size and power of the biggest banks has increased dramatically.

18- Bank market concentration and monopoly power: Has become more concentrated.

19- Adjustable Rate Mortgages (ARM's): Probably the biggest single cause of increased defaults as mortgage payments could jump as much as 50%, little to no change from bill.

20- Teaser rates: Still legal. Still a joke.

21- Low down payments required: Ads on radio still promoting the idea.

22- Personal bankruptcy law: Nothing done, judge needs authority to be able to adjust mortgage balance.

23- Regulating long maturity asset industries: Bank and insurance companies are long maturity asset and liability games with no short term implications to managements or their compensation from losses occurring long into the future. Needs special regulation of these markets but little has been done to address the problem.

24- Regulatory capture: The same, revolving door, industry groups and big money in politics writing our legislation and regulations, or in some cases, erasing them.

25- Managing risk: Need to separate principal investing, trading, investment banking and other risky activities within deposit taking commercial banks. No return to Glass Steagall or prohibition on these activities in the bill with the exception that foreign exchange, gold and silver trading will have to be done in a separate subsidiary or could be banned completely by banks.

26- Bankruptcy proceedings for banks and corporations:
Plan addressed for FDIC banks to liquidate quickly if overseas subsidiaries do not create a problem, which they will, but still have to create an accelerated process for all corporations so debtors as well as stockholders can take a hit to their poorly invested debt capital rather than bailing all creditors out at par.

27- Hedge funds: Still no investigation of their role as counter-party and enabler to a lot of bank and derivative nonsense, still no bill to tax their managers at ordinary rates rather than capital gain rates.

28- Management incentives: Still not complete, no one has asked why if bank executives were given long vesting stock options before, why weren't the managers thinking long term and thus be better aligned with shareholder perspective. Not just a question of when executive receives bonus, must also have skin in the game. All stock and options can't be free or executives have no downside to worry about and act like pure upside option holders.

29- Complexity of mortgage and investment banking products: Banks introduced complexity to products on purpose to confuse investors, to reduce competition and increase profit spreads. This ends up reducing liquidity. Very little of the real problem has been addressed.

30- Bad bank loans: Most still on banks' books and losses have not been realized. TARP was supposed to be used for this, but then Paulson decided not to. Fed trying desperate measures to hide bank problems on its balance sheet and eventually transfer the bad loans to Fannie and Freddie where they will never be seen again but taxpayer will pay for losses.

31- Government stimulus: Saved or created zero new or imaginary jobs, just an excuse to keep public employees fully employed. If state, local and federal governments hire and promote their workers during good times, but won't lay them off during bad times, how do we ever make government smaller and more efficient. Simple math tells you that under this formulation, eventually, everyone will be working for the government, I don't know how we will be able to pay our tax bill however.

32- Severity of new bank regulations: The stocks of the big banks went up on news that this financial reform package was going to pass. What does that tell you?

33- Bank executive compensation: The same, if not worse as the bonuses are just as big, but now there are losses at the banks rather than profits and much of this bonus pool money is coming directly from US taxpayer.

34- Undervalued Chinese currency: Extremely slow progress.

35- Globalization: Created vast inequality as American workers were forced to compete with workers from $1 an hour wage countries. Raghuram Rajan argues that inequality contributed to the financial crisis by encouraging our government (through Fannie and Freddie) to promote home ownership aggressively to make up for lost wages and benefits of the American worker. Globalization allowed US companies to avoid taxation and regulation (environmental, banking, disclosure, workplace rules, union rules, product safety, etc.) and geographic horizons of institutional and individual investors were stretched so far as to make investment analysis and supervision of management teams completely unmanageable.

36- Bank transparency: Probably worse given their derivative positions, their off-balance sheet shenanigans continue and the fact that all the new regulation and bank mergers means lots of restatements and footnotes and asterisks and fine print in the financial reports.

37- Externality costs and collective action problems: Very little progress, still don't know how you manage your risks and maintain market share when you as a banker are offering conventional 30 year fixed rate mortgages with a required 20% down payment to your customers and a new bank competitor opens across the street from you offering interest only, pay only if you feel like it, never repay the principal, zero down, zero closing costs, no income, no job, no problem, 2% teaser rate for five years, no prepayment penalty, no closing costs, feel free to take as much money out to buy that new car you always wanted, adjustable rate mortgages. Until long maturity industries like banking and insurance figure out this collective action problem and how to control it, they are doomed to these same crises in the future, The free market alone cannot address this unique type of problem where the dumbest makes the most and gains the most customers with losses postponed for decades.

38- Federal Reserve independence: We get a one-time partial audit and presidents of local boards no longer appointed by banks, but entire Fed continues to be dominated and controlled by banks and does their bidding rather than the people's.

39- Response times to crises: Our understanding of how to respond quickly and effectively to systemic financial crises hasn't improved. Not much learned, but we will get another chance real soon. Just look at the length of problems in this list and ask how many we really understand or believe we have solved for the future.

40- Underwater mortgage holders: No real help. Very few mortgage modifications. No mark downs of mortgage amounts. 25% of mortgages now underwater nationally where the mortgage balance is greater than the current home value and possibly as much as 50% of mortgages in California are already underwater.

41- Social Security (SS) and Medicare Impacts: Debt investor concerns on looming SS and Medicare blowup and potential insolvencies affects viability of entire financial system and the dollar. Not addressed by congress although it could be a $50 trillion problem that is a big enough number to cause the US to default on some obligations in the not too distant future.

42- The media: Corporate owned media dependent on corporate sponsored ads heavily biased on bullish buy side of market, always - Nothing's changed. CNBC never saw a stock they didn't like.

43- Insider trading and market manipulation: Policing and enforcement, especially at hedge funds, nothing to report.

44- Public reporting and transparency of publicly traded corporations: Derivative positions of $600 trillion notional amount make reading and analyzing an annual report almost meaningless as it is impossible to know the company's exposure to risky events and assets.

45- Overnight repo market: Nothing done to prevent funding of banks and investment banks with many long term obligations with overnight borrowings. Could mean the start of another possible run on the banks from their overnight lenders similar to what happened in this crisis.

46- Corruption in government: Two party system encourages collusion when investigating ethical and legal oversights, money in politics distorts all votes and gerrymandering election districts assures us that the Democrats and Republicans that survive their primaries will be so far to the right or left as to make cooperation and governance in Washington nearly impossible. Much of this crisis could have been avoided with more effective government supervision as market economies are poorly prepared to manage systemic risk, collective action problems, externalities and ethical questions a bank corporate charter has no opinion on. Corporations were created to make profits, governments were created to solve problems that markets have difficulty understanding. We are quickly becoming a banana republic where government and the media act as paid employees of oligarchs and big banks and corporations. We invented government and the corporate form, they are virtual entities, they exist only in documents in DC and in lawyer offices' filing cabinets, and yet now we find ourselves controlled by them, a true Frankenstein horror.

47- Global banking system: In worse shape now given that Europe has sovereign debt crisis to deal with. Just like the AAA layers of Collateralized Debt Obligations (CDOs) that European banks bought during the mortgage crisis and now are experiencing default rates of 93%, now we have trillions more of what were supposed to be AAA sovereign credits being held by the same European banks but represent countries with 14% government budget deficits (Greece), 20% unemployment (Spain), countries with banks that are eight times bigger than their entire GDP (Ireland) and whose populations are aging and retiring so rapidly they will not see big real GDP growth for generations. These countries, and many others in Europe, will certainly be downgraded significantly in the near future and outright government defaults are not out of the question. The problem is exasperated by the fact that Value at Risk (VAR) accounting allowed these European banks to hold AAA assets like CDOs and sovereign debt with almost infinite leverage so they have very little equity standing behind these loans which means once again that the taxpayers throughout all the countries of Europe, and the US, will be picking up the tab when these countries do default or restructure their debt.

Chapter 13

Written in March 2011

When Corporations and Banks Ruled the World

Can you have a conspiracy if the conspirators hardly ever talk to each other and rarely ever meet? Certainly, not in the traditional sense of the word. But very large corporations acting only in their narrow self-interest are completing a takeover of our government, our media, our academic institutions and policy institutes, our jobs and our hearts and minds better than a well oiled conspiracy. We shall see that their shared belief that maximizing their own profitability is best for society was sufficient to accomplish much of this takeover. I am not saying they don't cozy up and cooperate and collude at their industry conferences, their Chamber of Commerce meetings and their Business Roundtable discussions. Only, that it may not be necessary.

The path to total global domination by big corporations was self evident once we allowed entities such as corporations into the political arena given that, by law, they have but one motive, maximizing profits and shareholder value. This approach, that has worked so well in the economic marketplace fails miserably when we allow corporations to make societal and ethical decisions typically reserved for individuals. It will always be in the interest of big for profit corporations, if they think they can get away with it to mislead customers, to defraud investors, to rip off consumers, to pollute the environment, to bribe Congressmen, to hire illegals, to lie in advertisements, to bust unions, to underpay their workers and to not fund their pensions. Why? Because it increases profits. That is why we have government and regulation. So big corporations and others can't cheat. So they are forced to play fair.

There is a libertarian school of thought that says no regulation of business is necessary because the corporation's concern for its own reputation will always lead it to a moral path. The financial crisis proved otherwise as executives of 100-year-old banking institutions acted unethically and criminally to maximize their own compensation even if it meant tarnishing the reputation of their firm. Even if we properly supervised managements of banks and other corporate entities, shareholders themselves don't mind risking the reputation of their corporate entities if the payoff is big enough and they have lots of leverage to maximize their gains.

Alan Greenspan went so far as to believe that fraud by corporations should not be prosecuted, believing instead that no corporate executive would ever commit a fraudulent act and risk endangering his firm's reputation. How someone with this crazy belief system became our nation's top bank regulator is incredible. It wasn't by accident. I believe he was chosen by his supporters in the banking industry for exactly this reason. They knew he would do nothing to stop their fraudulent and criminal mistreatment of their customers and investors.

The takeover by big corporations and banks in the world is pervasive. I am not saying that all corporations are bad and I am not making an argument against capitalism, per se. But I believe, for society to be most productive and its citizens happiest and most fulfilled it is appropriate to ask big corporations to restrict their activities to the economic marketplace and avoid their frequent excursions into our politics, our government, our free speech and our national discourse.

I would hope that many of you who work for big corporations come to see the logic of my argument and don't take it as a threat to your livelihood. I want to see you prosper, but I want you to do it based on your corporation's competitive strength in the economic marketplace, not in its ability to lobby and bribe our elected officials. When I find fault with a particular industry such as the defense industry, I am not arguing to do away with the industry, just to reform it, and the people working in that industry are the most qualified to fix the problem.

Corporate Dominance of the Economic Marketplace

Corporations were formed to compete in the economic marketplace. But even the economic marketplace has seen vast consolidation in which entire industries, especially on a regional basis, have been reduced to a handful of very large corporations. There are many companies that enjoy outright monopoly power and many other industries that are so concentrated in so few hands that collusion and price-fixing is quite easy to achieve. Marketing professors will tell you that price-fixing can occur through price signaling without the need for a single telephone conversation between industry leaders.

Corporate Dominance in the Defense Industry

I understand I will make few new friends by criticizing our defense industry. Please remember that I'm criticizing the defense business, not our men and women in uniform. Like the healthcare industry, the defense industry works closely with our government and is dependent on it for a large percentage of its revenues.

The US spends six times as much on defense as any other country, more than the next six countries' defense budgets combined. What do we have to show for it? We have lost wars in Vietnam, Korea, Iraq and Afghanistan. This sounds like some kind of a joke. The world's greatest economic and military power can't defeat the world's smallest and poorest countries in war. We bankrupted Iraq in our first war with them and still couldn't win Iraq II.

I assure you it is not because our opponent's fighting personnel are braver than our own or somehow more committed to the cause. I don't think it was an accident that it has taken us decades to defeat these third world nations. I believe it was purposeful, if not to lose, to so drag out these wars over such a long period of time that our country remained in a constant state of war, similar to the constant battling and never ending war in the novel *1984* between Oceania, Eurasia and Eastasia.

I believe our biggest corporate weapons manufacturers and defense companies want war to go on indefinitely because it is profitable to them. They know not to wage war with the more powerful countries on earth because they are some of our biggest trading partners. Non-defense corporations, who are also motivated by profits and have enormous political influence would object if we started bombing their biggest suppliers and customers overseas.

So we purposely chose bankrupt, Third World, barely-developing nations to make war with. But that is not the worst of it. We stretch the conflict out forever with no end in sight so the defense companies have a ready market to sell their weapons to.

In Vietnam, we found that the American people did not approve of losing 58,000 American fighting men and women to a meaningless war. So in Iraq and Afghanistan, we perfected the model of a never-ending war by drastically limiting large-scale engagements and battles with the enemy where the loss of life might threaten public support for the conflicts. In Iraq, approximately half of our casualties were caused by friendly fire and of the remaining half, more than 60% occurred in the transporting of troops rather than in battle.

Halliburton, the company where Dick Cheney was CEO, acquired a no-bid, non-compete contract from our government to offer all subcontract services in Iraq during the war. This resulted in a literal gravy train to Halliburton as they charged us $75 for a G.I. breakfast consisting of scrambled eggs, a biscuit with gravy and a piece of bacon, something any Denny's can get you for about $3.75. Halliburton stock increased 600% during the Iraq war.

The defense establishment always needs a villain to justify its big defense expenditures. When the Soviet Republic fell and communist China turned to capitalism, the defense business was in desperate need of a new villain. They have created one in Islam. There are 1.2 billion peaceful Muslims on this planet and prior to our invasion of Iraq and Afghanistan probably less than 200,000 wished serious harm to the United States. Al Qaida members, prior to our invasion of Afghanistan and Iraq, numbered less than a couple thousand worldwide. Now, the number of Muslims that wishes us harm is measured in the tens of millions thanks to our overly aggressive response to 9/11, something the defense establishment is thrilled about. Without an enemy, they are out of business. If they can get Americans to fear all Muslims in the world they will be in business for a long time to come.

It's not just the defense industry that benefits from war. As we have expanded our mission in these countries to peacekeeping, policymaking, infrastructure rebuilding and nation building we find that private security companies like Blackwater and construction companies like Bechtel do awfully well by war also. The defense establishment did a very smart thing. Instead of battling with the non-defense companies over whether global peace or global war is best for profits, it cut many of them in on the terrible, but enormous profits of war.

Corporate Dominance in the Labor Market

Another purely economic marketplace that has been dominated by the power of very large corporations is the labor market. Union membership has declined from 35% of our total workforce to just 9% today. Even the word "union" has obtained some sort of negative connotation like the words "wealth redistribution" or "global warming".

What would the world be like without unions? Would you like to go back to a union-free environment? It is easy to do so. Just visit China. They don't allow independent unions there, but they do allow underage girls living ten to a room, two to a bunk, to work twelve hours a day, seven days a week for less than one dollar per hour with no benefits, no healthcare, no pension and no hopes of an adequate education in workplaces that are unsafe and sometimes deadly.

Corporate Domination of Our Government

Of course the greatest impact big corporations have exerted, and the most misplaced, is on our government representatives. I don't need to spend a lot of time here because it has been the focus of much of the rest of this book. It cannot be a good idea to allow your government, whose job it is to focus on ethical, fairness, justice and community issues to be taken over by big corporations that have but one incentive, solely the maximization of profits. Corporations are great in the economic marketplace playing a game called capitalism, but the game requires a rulebook, and in democratic societies the only legitimate moral power to make those rules comes from the people through their elected representatives in the political arena, an area corporations should be prohibited from entering.

Joe Stiglitz properly points out that basic human rights arguments as well as our constitution give people the right to speak freely, to assemble and to petition their government. Corporations have no natural or moral rights and are not referenced in the constitution. Corporations are legal entities that we created, they are completely virtual, they are not human. We decide when we write their articles of incorporation what rights we will give them. But we reserve all sorts of rights from them. They don't have a right to life, we can close them in bankruptcy. They don't have a right to a pursuit of happiness nor would they understand it if we granted it to them.

We decided that it would be beneficial to society if they could have a right to acquire property, but that was our decision, not granted from some higher moral authority or the constitution. So, we wouldn't be violating any law, stated or otherwise, if we decided to limit corporations' ability to lobby the government, contribute to candidates for office or advertise during campaigns. We can't prevent people from forming an association as a corporation, but it does not give that corporation the right to lobby our government if the express purpose of that association is purely economic, the maximization of shareholder value. A group of employees or a group of shareholders can form an association for lobbying purposes, but the corporation itself, formed solely for economic purposes is not a valid human entity with such rights.

Corporate Dominance of Our Political Parties

As any eighth grader can tell you, our democracy is stable because of its checks and balances. It is almost impossible to imagine a corporate takeover of our government without some warning or whistle blowing by another institution initially created to protect our freedoms.

The first such institution I can think of is our two-party political system. If one party or one of its members were taking bribes in the form of campaign contributions or lobbyist donations, surely the other party would blow the whistle. It now appears obvious that both political parties are taking cash for votes. Candidates take money to get elected or reelected given the high cost of television advertising. We cannot expect either political party to lead the charge for reform since both parties have their heads stuck deeply into this illicit trough of money.

Corporate Dominance of Our Media

The next institution we turn to protect us and our freedoms if both political parties lose their way is the free press. Media has become a business itself now, but we must also remember that it is a vital component of a free and democratic society. In my previous academic research we found that a free press is not only essential to preserving a democracy, it is also a critical component of a healthy and growing economy.

Almost all of the larger radio stations, all the major network and cable news channels, almost all of our major newspapers and magazines as well as all of our major book publishing houses are now owned by large corporations. As recently as 30 years ago, many of these media outlets were owned by entrepreneurs and family businesses. It is not healthy for a country to have its entire media owned by the government either, but allowing it to be held in private hands removes a major watchdog on our democracy if corporations decide to take on Washington.

Corporate Dominance of Academia

Another watchdog of our democracy that has been compromised recently is our academia, especially our finance, business and economics professors. We grant professors tenure and lifetime employment to assure them independence with a hope that a lack of bias in their research and public statements will be preserved. But now, many of these economics professors receive multiples of their teaching salary from outside work with corporations. Speaking engagements, expert witness testimony consulting assignments, corporate partnerships and corporate junkets all provide the opportunity for a financial conflict of interest. I believe this is the major reason no economist sounded the alarm about this pending financial crisis. They are sponsored by, and partners with, the very hedge funds, commercial banks and investment banks that were the primary cause of this crisis.

Even now, many professors are working overtime to try to create a scenario in which it was not the banks that caused this crisis. Rather it was big government and an irrational citizenry. They point the finger at Fannie Mae and Freddie Mac thinking they are agencies of the government, not realizing they are for-profit corporations who pay their top executives hundreds of millions of dollars in bonuses, have publicly traded stock and stock options for their executives and were the biggest lobbyists and contributors to the Congress over the last 20 years.

We have seen that in addition to corporate attempts to infiltrate our universities, they also created their own faux-academic institutions. Known inappropriately as think tanks, these policy institutes provide educational materials for our elected representatives and the media, never disclosing that their funding comes from large corporations, wealthy individuals and the defense industry. These policy institutes attract second-tier academics who could not find jobs in academia and whose research papers would never be accepted by prominent peer-reviewed independent academic journals. But their views are reported by the media as factual and well researched and unbiased without ever disclosing their obvious conflicts of interest.

Corporate Dominance in Our Society

If corporations really ruled the world, what would this world look like? Consumption would be emphasized over everything as this is the primary driver of corporate profits. Status seeking would be encouraged as it promotes never-ending consumption in an impossible attempt to constantly one-up your neighbors and friends. Teenagers, rather than wearing jerseys and caps of their favorite baseball team would wear apparel with corporate names like Abercrombie and Fitch or Nike stitched, not on the inside of their shirts, but on the outside.

Children as young as three would demand that their mothers buy apparel and toys embossed with corporate sponsored characters such as Barbie and Winnie the Pooh even though it costs 3 to 5 times as much as similar generic merchandise.

All forms of debt including credit card debt, auto loans, consumer loans, payday loans, mortgages, second mortgages and home equity loans would be encouraged because the corporation needs sales now even if the consumer has to go into suffocating debt in order to keep the corporate profits churning.

If corporations ruled the world, they would encourage government representatives to vote for lower corporate taxes, increased subsidies and tax loopholes for corporations, lower personal income taxes for their wealthiest executives and capital gains taxed at a lower rate than ordinary income. Government would be encouraged to privatize everything including Social Security as this would create more opportunities for corporate America to grow.

Almost all government expenditures on behalf of taxpayers would quickly find their way back into corporate hands. Tax money directed to supposedly save failing economies like the $50 billion given Mexico in 1995 would find its way back into the New York bank's vaults within 24 hours. Any foreign aid to the developing world and any military aid extended to a foreign country would have stipulations attached that the money had to be spent on goods, machinery and weapons produced by American corporations. What appeared to be a benefit to the elderly of George W. Bush offering to pay their pharmaceutical bills through Medicare would actually be a corporate devised plan to keep pharmaceutical prices high and allow them to be funded by the younger generation.

If corporations ruled the world, corporations and banks would be announcing record profits and paying their executives record bonuses in this crisis even as ordinary Americans face record levels of joblessness, foreclosures and asset loss. The DOW would recover thanks to government intervention in the economy; economists would claim the recession was officially over even though average families continued to struggle paying bills with paychecks that had not increased in thirty years. Both parents would have to find work to afford basic necessities like a home, a car and food and healthcare for their children.

If corporations ruled the world, important issues to ordinary Americans would never be addressed by our government. Our schools would decay, our environment would suffer, crime would continue, poverty would increase, jobs would disappear overseas, illegals would force wages down at home, our homes would be foreclosed and our savings and pensions eliminated.

Aren't you glad you don't live in such a corporate dominated society?

Chapter 14

Written in March 2011

What Does the Future Hold?

Each time that I write a book, I hope that times have changed, that we have learned from our errors of the past, that the people have finally awoken from their stupor and become involved and just once I could paint a rosy picture of the future.

It hurts me to say this is not the case today. Corporate dominance is as strong as ever, with corporations now having sunk their claws even into our Supreme Court. While the tea party is a populist uprising of angry Americans, its libertarian prescription of less government and less regulation is just what the corporations ordered. The Obama administration has proven once again that it doesn't matter which party is in power, the banks' are calling the shots. I am sure the word "change" means different things to different people, but the change I voted for with Obama was to throw the lobbyists out of Washington and get the money out of politics. We have seen that the financial reform legislation recently enacted is toothless when it comes to regulating the banks. Most tellingly, there have been no arrests of bankers and politicians who were complicit in the creation of this crisis. If we do not learn from the past we are doomed to repeat it.

Because we have not addressed the fundamental causes of the crisis, we will face even greater crises in the future. They will grow to such a magnitude that they will eventually grab our attention.

There are lots of problems that remain unresolved, but the biggest by far is how out of control the governments of the world are and how beholding they are to corporate special interests. Corporations want governments to spend, either to artificially stimulate the economy to keep consumers buying or just so corporations can grab a meaningful percentage of government spending as their revenue source. Government defense spending, Medicare expenditures, corporate subsidies, price supports, corporate tax breaks, even money government gives the unemployed and the elderly all ends up eventually in corporate hands. So corporations are the last entities that want to see government spending curtailed. And this government spending in support of greater corporate revenues is creating unmanageable debt loads on almost all of the advanced countries of the world.

Globally, the richest countries on earth, Japan, the US and the European countries including the UK are all at a phase in their history when the great majority of their citizens, the baby-boomers, are about to retire. This is no surprise. Demographic experts have been watching this age bubble percolate through their age distribution charts since its inception just after World War II.

But, we have not planned accordingly. It was apparent to all that when these hard-working, well-educated, highly motivated baby boomers retired we would see a dramatic reduction in output and growth in the economy and a commensurate reduction in tax revenue to fund our governments. Second, it was well understood that these baby boomers would soon exhaust their savings and caring for them would become a huge cost burden to the governments of the world. Finally, these baby boomers are living longer and consuming greater quantities of ever more costly medicine and medical procedures each year. The fastest-growing group, those over 80 years old are the most costly to care for.

Anyone can tell you that if you see such a huge cost burden and revenue loss occurring in an advanced economy the only sensible thing to do is to save money now to fund some of the cost later. That is what we tried to do, at least on paper, by building up surpluses in our Social Security and Medicare trust funds. But as soon as the cash arrived, the government borrowed it for general operating purposes, a great percentage of which ended up in corporate hands.

So the money is gone. If instead of holding US government debt securities, the trust funds had invested in gold, for example, they would not only still have this money, it would have protected its purchasing power. It is as if we created a bank vault to hold monies for the express purpose of housing, feeding and caring of the sick and elderly and then allowed corporations to pick the lock, rob the bank and make off with all the proceeds.

The next big crisis on the horizon is what the corporations left behind in exchange for raiding our government of all its money, IOUs. Not IOUs of the corporations, but rather IOUs of the government itself. In essence, governments borrowed from future generations, not to provide care for their sick and elderly, but rather to inflate the revenues and profits of our biggest corporations. And now that very debt is strangling these countries' governments as they try to find ways of paying the ever increasing interest on that debt.

It is this explosion of government debt in the world that will trigger the next crisis. Like the debt in the mortgage crisis, most sovereign country debt is rated AAA so no investor will expect major defaults, especially among the more advanced countries of the world. The amount of sovereign debt in the world, currently approximately $35 trillion and on its way very quickly to $50 trillion, will make the $3 trillion subprime mortgage crisis seem like a minor tremor compared to the major devastating economic earthquake to come.

It is not just governments that are in trouble. Citizens around the world have not saved enough for their retirements. One, most corporations terminated the defined benefit pension plans for their employees over the last 20 years in an attempt to increase corporate profits and shift investment risk from their balance sheets to their employees. Two, Americans have done a poor job of adding to their 401(k) retirement plans as the median balance of a 401(k) today is about $12,000, hardly enough to retire on. Three, many people around the world presumed they could retire on the equity they had built up in their homes. This, thanks to the housing crash is no longer true. Many homeowners have seen their home equity evaporate as now one in four Americans have homes that are underwater, that is the house is worth less than the mortgage. Four, many Americans over 55 years of age are being laid off in this recession and cannot find other work, further straining their retirement plans.

I don't think people realize how widespread the government sovereign debt crisis is going to be. We have all heard about Greece, Iceland, Ireland, Portugal and Spain, but as I demonstrated in Chapter 11, it is the biggest, richest and most advanced countries of the world that will be tested the most. It is the advanced countries' banks that have lent these troubled sovereign credits money and it will be their governments who have to go into further debt to bail out both the countries that get into trouble as well as the banks in the advanced countries that lent to them.

So this current financial crisis could not have come at a worse time for these countries struggling to deal with their excessive debts. One, it has put the world's largest banks in jeopardy at a time when their governments are already running significant operating deficits due to the recession. This means that any attempt by the governments to rescue the troubled banks will have to be done by issuing additional new debt thus contributing to even higher debt to GDP percentages for these countries.

Two, the very notion of a global recession/depression is that high unemployment and lower business activity results in less government tax revenue. This lower tax revenue creates deficits that add to the levels of sovereign debt. If we are slow to emerge from the current financial crisis, as I expect, then these ongoing deficits will dramatically increase sovereign debt worldwide by trillions of dollars.

Three, the current crisis has impacted the ability of countries to repay their debts which means their cost of borrowing will increase in real terms to reflect this greater risk. The cost of borrowing will increase as well in nominal terms if these countries decide to print money to fund their deficits as inflation returns. This means that we can expect governments to carry increased interest expense on their debt loads going forward. If the cost of borrowing for the U.S. Treasury goes from 3% to 10% because of an increased fear of future inflation combined with paying a higher default premium, this will add an additional $1 trillion to the annual deficit making it impossible for Congress to balance the budget and thus reduce or stabilize debt loads in the future.

A rough cut rule of thumb is that countries typically get into trouble when their total debt exceeds their entire GDP. The US, France, Germany and the UK, as well as most of the other European countries will very quickly exceed this dangerous threshold in the very near future. Japan is already there. The great recession and its associated government operating deficits will last much longer than people expect, banks will continue to write off bad loans that will require local government support and the baby boom retirement will dramatically decrease government tax revenues while at the same time putting enormous demands on governments to provide for the retirement and healthcare of their elderly citizens.

As far as investment advice goes, there is no country debt or country currency that I would like to hold right now. Similarly, there are no commercial or residential real estate assets I would like to own. The only exception, if you find yourself in a town that has had house price declines of some 40% to 60% from the peak and you can borrow mortgage monies on a fixed rate basis for 30 years at less than 6% and you are sure you are going to live in the house for at least 15 years, then you might consider buying today. The home you purchase is unlikely to grow in price faster than general inflation, but if your debt costs are locked in and inflation comes roaring back, you could easily make 10 to 20 times your equity investment of say, 15% of the total value of the house.

In 2008, in a book I wrote called *Contagion*, I recommended people buy Chinese stocks, TIPS and gold. Immediately thereafter, Chinese stocks increased by more than 40%, gold prices nearly doubled and an investment in TIPS would have protected your purchasing power, something a typical bank CD failed to do.

I still like TIPS and gold as hedges against unexpected inflation, but I would be hesitant at these price levels that are approaching $1,400 an ounce to put all my money into gold. Gold certainly has a chance of reaching $2,000 or even $3000 an ounce, and it also has the potential to drop to $700 an ounce. Gold has already made a significant move reflecting the dramatic increase by the Federal Reserve in printing additional reserves. At this time it would be smarter to invest in real assets that have not shown as dramatic appreciation today as gold. That is why TIPS are so attractive. They don't pay off until the higher inflation is realized, and if we are wrong and deflation persists, recently issued TIPS trading at par can provide a partial hedge even against this risk.

The only big risk with TIPS is if the US government cheats and doesn't pay out the real inflation rate. They have lots of ways of doing this, all quite corrupt, but I wouldn't put it past them at least trying. The simplest is to just change how the CPI index is calculated. In fact, they have already done that in the recent past by allowing higher priced goods to be substituted out of the assumed basket of purchased goods, a change which causes reported CPI to decline relative to actual price increases.

The Solution

The solution to the problem is not simple, nor is it easy. The problem is immense and global so we should not pretend that there is an easy answer. The reform movement is going to have to come from outside Washington as both political parties, the congress, the president and even the Supreme Court are totally corrupted by corporate influence.

I've always thought that my best idea to make corporations understand the damage they are doing with their lobbying, and that they are powerless without us, the consumers, would be to start a website called something like www.boycott.com (I know – the name's taken). I have not found the time to begin such an effort, but I would be very happy if someone reading this grabbed the ball and ran with it to get the website started.

The concept is to attract 1 million or 5 million or 10 million Americans to the website through advertising, e-mails or through a social networking sites like Facebook or Twitter. Word of mouth promotion among supporters of the idea would have to be the most cost effective means of rapidly growing the site. Then, each month the website would announce to its members the most egregious corporation with regard to the lobbying or corrupting of our government. If visitors to the website stop buying that corporation's products and told their friends not to purchase products from that corporation, I believe a new consumer movement could be inaugurated.

This is a wonderfully powerful weapon against corporate abuse. Fundamentalist Christians in the US have used it against the consumer product companies by threatening to stop buying the product of those companies that continue to advertise on television programs that exhibit explicit sex and violence. Even though the membership of these organizations only numbers in the hundreds of thousands, they have made a real impact on television content in a country of 300 million people.

When I tell people my idea of www.boycott.com they immediately realize how difficult it will be to get started, but there is no better time than now and there is real money out there that I believe would be interested in backing such an effort. But people's objection to the idea is almost always the same. They don't think we can get to the biggest companies and they don't know how we would boycott a Bank of America or Goldman Sachs. Trust me, if people started cutting up there Bank of America credit cards like draft dodgers used to tear up their draft cards back in the 60s we would have the beginnings of a powerful new movement. Getting to Goldman Sachs which mostly deals with large companies and institutional investors would be more difficult, but remember the anti-apartheid movement that pressured investors to disinvest themselves of their stock holdings in South Africa. A letter writing campaign to our banks, insurance companies, labor unions and pension funds asking them not to deal with Goldman Sachs until it stops its lobbying efforts might be a good place to start.

Even if, God willing, we have some success and corporations pull back their lobbying and campaign contributions, it is hard to see this Supreme Court ever limiting corporations ability to run television ads during campaigns. It smells too much like book burning to the Supreme Court. So the ultimate responsibility lies with us. We must see that our children become well enough educated that they know how to critically evaluate new information in a campaign ad and they must learn to ask the most basic of questions like who is paying for the ad? An effort to improve our public school system will be rewarded by providing an educated electorate much less likely to vote against its own economic interests based on the lies and deceptions of a corporate sponsored advertising campaign. I understand this potential solution has a very long-term timeframe, but please realize, this problem is not going away anytime soon.

This next proposed solution will separate the summer soldier and sunshine patriot from those combatants ready to take a strong stand in this battle for our country. I would ask each of you to turn off your televisions. Not only do corporate sponsored and owned television news programs completely distort the issues and only provide a pro-corporate message, the real danger of television is that it creates a pablum-spewing, saliva-drooling, near-comatose and completely passive electorate ill-prepared to defend its civil liberties. The million-dollar question during this financial crisis is why haven't more people gotten out and gone into the streets to protest the loss of their jobs, their homes and their savings. I think the answer is because they were stuck in the cushions of their lazy boy recliners in front of the TV watching there can't-miss episodes of *The Amazing Race*, *Survivor* and *American Idol*.

Short of actually rioting in the street, concerned citizens can do a whole lot of good by not only voting out corrupt incumbents, but also by forming new political parties. The progressive wing of the Democratic Party must form a Tea Party movement of its own to try to clean up the corporate influence and corruption in the Democratic Party. Its platform does not have to be complicated. Solely, it needs to return the Democratic Party to the people. A similar effort could be started to organize independents who have grown tired of both political parties. People registered as independent now outnumber those registered as Republicans or Democrats. I would vote for Elizabeth Warren or Bill Gates or Warren Buffet or Michael Bloomberg for president on an independent ticket if they would just agree that their main focus will be getting control of the corporate influence in Washington. The billionaires could put some muscle behind their resolution by agreeing to forfeit half their net worth if they fail to try to accomplish that mission once they are elected.

I would keep the charter of the new political party quite simple as the more things you suggest you are in favor of, the more supporters you will lose. People don't vote for policy initiatives they like, people vote against policies they don't like. I don't believe you have to announce that the new party is antiwar or pro-education or pro-environment. Once you get corporate special interest money sidelined I think you'll find that almost all Americans support these positions. I would try to keep it very simple, against corporate campaign donations and lobbying and against gerrymandering. The movement has to start on the Internet as it is the last bastion of freedom in the media. What is needed is more than just simple blogging. Right now, many bloggers do more harm than good by being so overly critical of new ideas that supportive contributors retreat and decide not to communicate over the Internet. There are obvious problems with every approach, but at some point it takes more courage to sign on as a follower than as a leader.

So if none of this works, is there an ultimate nuclear option? I believe there is. I think it is appropriate for many homeowners to stop making payments on their mortgages. It is easy to demonstrate that the run-up in prices during the housing price bubble was caused by a conspiracy of lenders, mortgage brokers, real estate agents, appraisers, commercial banks, investment banks, rating agencies, middlemen, regulators and our elected representatives. Prices never would have gotten to these unsustainable levels if it were not for this conspiracy. What happened was criminal. It makes no sense for a homeowner to continue to try to fund a home purchase that was accomplished at a non-market price that was inflated due to criminal behavior. Please remember, a homeowner always has the option to default on his or her mortgage. You have been paying a premium on your interest rate to acquire just this option. It is completely legal and it is completely moral. Think how nice it would be to unload the headaches of an underwater mortgage and go rent for a while. People seem obsessed with homeownership but I'm not sure they properly weigh the stress and pressures it creates in knowing that if they miss one mortgage payment they can lose their home.

I would go further than that. I would stop payment on major credit cards and tear them up. Your credit rating will be damaged for some time, but that is okay, especially if lots of people join in. The personal credit rating system is a scam anyway in which negative information can be added to your report with no review by you. Errors in the report are almost impossible to correct. Minor incidences like a single late payment or even a request to see your credit score can negatively impact that score.

The entire credit rating process is nothing more than an attempt to get poor and middle-class people to pay a higher price for goods and services than the wealthy. Automobiles are advertised for $200 a month, but the salesman makes you feel guilty by telling you that your credit score is not perfect and so for you the payments will be $350 a month. What he fails to tell you is that almost no one has a credit score high enough to qualify for the $200 per month payment plan for the automobile. A rich person buys a 21" LCD TV for $200 and a poor person rents the same TV at a Rent-a-Center for three years at a total cost of $1,200.

If you want to put the fear of God in corporations show them you don't want their credit, you don't want to borrow any more money, you may not pay back what you have already borrowed and you certainly don't plan on buying as much junk that sits on the shelves in the stores in every mall in America as you have in the past.

Finally there is the ultimate threat. I don't suggest that I condone it, partly because if I did I would be liable for treason and my next book would be penned with a pen from a pen, penitentiary that is. The ultimate threat to a corrupt government is to threaten to stop paying your taxes. We haven't come to that yet in this crisis, but judging how incredibly corrupt our government is one can conclude that that day may not be that far off in the future.

I used to think that to start a political movement it made sense to make the first step so easy that anyone could do it with little effort or commitment. I tried that once and all I attracted were summer soldiers who might e-mail or blog but would never consider taking any more serious steps or actions.

Maybe the way to start a political movement is by appealing to the bravest to take a very bold step like suspending the payments on his or her debts or stop paying taxes. You will attract significantly fewer supporters, but just maybe others will recognize their bravery and decide to follow. Not that I am advocating it, but remember, the Egyptian revolt was started by a street vendor who refused to pay bribes to government officials and instead lit himself on fire.

I hope it never comes to an all-out tax revolt. I hope we can find some way to clean up our government and free it from corporate special interests with something short of this, but it does reinforce one very important point. Just as corporations and banks cannot survive without our purchasing their products and services, our corrupt government cannot survive without our taxes. The people have to come to understand that the ultimate power, both politically and economically resides with them.

It is incredible that the cost of a crisis caused entirely by bankers, corrupt lobbyists and corrupt politicians is being carried on the backs of working men and women, the unemployed, the elderly and the disadvantaged. Even after the crisis, bankers are now paying themselves record bonuses as the world's citizens suffer a loss of 50 million jobs, 20 million homes and approximately $30 trillion of accumulated wealth.

It is incredible that even after suffering these losses, the people of the world have not organized better to fight back.. I almost titled this book, "While America Slept" as I still can't believe the enormous suffering and pain that our citizens have experienced and how little protest and fight is in them. I thought the first step to getting people organized and in the streets was to get them angry at what had happened. My previous books attempted to do this. But we have to tread lightly. There is a thin line between anger and depression. It can be very depressing to realize how we are being taken advantage of and how little recourse we have to level the playing field. Once depression hits, it is very hard to find the energy to organize, boycott, protest or march.

It has been incredible to watch the world's leading democracy wither and shrink away. Whoever said that the real threat to America was internal, that our demise would not be the result of a foreign power had it right. Maybe what is lacking in America is a sense of moral outrage. Maybe, as a people we have lost our moral compass.

It is incredible to watch the world's great democracies trend toward default and bankruptcy. Future generations will scarce believe that people in Europe and America who not 60 years ago were threatened with fascism and the end of liberal democratic freedom would so endanger its future by allowing their corporate controlled governments to amass such massive government debts.

Finally, in my heart I remain optimistic. As Gandhi says, throughout history there have been tyrants and dictators, but in the long run the way of truth and love always prevails. It may take longer than we want but I have great confidence in Americans and the

206

peoples of the world that this injustice shall not stand. Remember, we created corporations and governments. They are virtual entities existing only in our minds and the people remain the only real force for good in the world. The people, united, will never be defeated.

CPSIA information can be obtained at www.ICGtesting.com
Printed in the USA
238758LV00004B/51/P